THE EMPEROR CONSTANTINE

THE EMPEROR
CONSTANTINE

A Chronicle

BY

DOROTHY L. SAYERS

WILLIAM B. EERDMANS PUBLISHING COMPANY
GRAND RAPIDS, MICHIGAN

Printed in the United States of America

First Published August 1951
This American Edition Published February 1976

Library of Congress Cataloging in Publication Data

Sayers, Dorothy Leigh, 1893-1957.
    The Emperor Constantine : a chronicle.

    Reprint of the ed. published by Gollancz, London.
    1. Constantinus I, the Great, Emperor of Rome,
d. 337—Drama. I. Title.
PR6037.A95E5 1976   822'.9'12   75-46543
ISBN 0-8028-3487-6

PREFACE

The reign of Constantine the Great is a turning-point in the history of Christendom. Those thirty years, from A.D. 306, when he was proclaimed Augustus by the Army of Britain at York, to A.D. 337, when, sole Emperor of the civilized world, he died at Nicomedia in Asia Minor, exchanging the Imperial purple for the white robe of his baptism, saw the emergence of the Christian ecclesia from the status of a persecuted sect to power and responsibility as the State Church of the Roman Empire. More important still, and made possible by that change of status, was the event of A.D. 325: the Council of Nicaea. At that first Great Synod of East and West, the Church declared her mind as to the Nature of Him whom she worshipped. By the insertion of a single word in the baptismal symbol of her faith, she affirmed that That which had been Incarnate at Bethlehem in the reign of Augustus Cæsar, suffered under Pontius Pilate, and risen from death in the last days of Tiberius was neither deified man, nor angel, nor demi-god, nor any created being however exalted, but Very God of Very God, co-equal and co-eternal with the Father.

The first Christian Emperor was thus, in the economy of Providence, the instrument whereby Christendom was brought face to face with two problems which have not yet found their full resolution: the exterior relations between Church and State; the interior relation between orthodox and heretic within the Church. It has long been fashionable to lay the blame on Constantine for the corruptions incidental to any alliance of the spiritual and temporal powers—for the rise of secularism and institutionalism within the City of God—for the unedifying spectacle of a Church compromising on the one hand with the world and on the other hand employing the arm of the State to police and persecute her own dissident members. But such criticism is scarcely helpful. The problem of power is not to be evaded; the changes were in the nature of things inevitable, and would have come about in course of time, if not by Constantine then by some other means. If the Gospel was to be "preached unto every creature", then Christianity must some day cease to be the cult of a minority, and the power of purse and sword must eventually come into Christian hands—as indeed the Lord Himself had told His disciples that they must. And sooner or later the Church must needs use her intellect to define her faith, lest identity be lost, and the truth once delivered to the Saints be merged in the welter of

5

Gnostic and semi-pagan cults which proliferated upon the decaying remnants of Hellenistic philosophy and the old religions.

Of the man about whom the Church and Empire thus crystallised into a new formation much is known; yet all that is known remains in a manner ambiguous. Posterity has called him "the Great"; yet his claim to greatness is as vigorously denied by some historians as it is affirmed by others. He spoke of himself as the vicegerent chosen by God to establish Christ's Empire on earth; yet he himself remained unbaptised until shortly before his death, and opinion is sharply divided upon the sincerity of his Christian profession. Was Christianity for him a living faith, a profitable superstition, or a cynical instrument of policy? It is certain that he took pains, in his middle life, to instruct himself in theology, and that in the Great Council he threw all his influence upon the side of the Catholic party; yet in his latter years he appeared to favour the Arian heretics, and banished that stormy petrel, the great Athanasius, whose doctrine had triumphed at Nicaea. The moment of his most splendid fortunes is darkened by the slaying of his wife and his brilliant young son and heir—madness, murder, an act of justice? No explanation that has been offered appears wholly satisfactory. The playwright, groping among the lights and shadows of history, must interpret the facts as best he may, so as to distil from them a reasonable and consistent story.

That story opens in the political chaos following upon the retirement of Diocletian, the great reforming statesman who had held the unwieldy and disintegrating Empire for twenty years in a precarious stability. The iron grip once relaxed, the wars of succession break out. Rival claimants to the twin imperial thrones of East and West fight, chase, murder one another between the Euxine and the Pillars of Hercules, and on both sides of the Middle Sea. In one confused year there are six rival emperors at once. Through the medley of names and fortunes, a steady progress becomes discernible. Constantine is moving east: from Britain to Gaul, from Gaul to Rome. Maxentius, Emperor of the West, goes out to meet him at the pass of the Red Rocks: he is confronted by soldiers bearing upon their shields a new and mysterious sign—the Greek letters Chi and Ro combined into a monogram. The Romans are trapped between two armies and beaten back with heavy slaughter to the Milvian Bridge. Maxentius is killed; Constantine enters the city in triumph and is acknowledged by the Senate as Emperor of the West. He gives thanks for victory to the One God; he annuls the edicts of persecution against the Christians, and advances them to riches and honour; the strange sign blazes in jewels and gold upon his banners; Rome beholds with astonishment and some disgust the portent of a Christian Emperor. The year is 312.

Twelve years later, Licinius, the pagan Emperor of the East, is beaten by sea in the Hellespont and by land at Chrysopolis in Asia Minor. Constantine enters Nicomedia, sole Emperor of East and West. He calls the Great Council of Nicaea, he moves the seat of Empire to Byzantium, which is rebuilt as a Christian city and renamed Constantinople.

His later years are embittered by the persistent repercussions of the Arian schism: the Church, purse and sword at her disposal, becomes, in her turn, a persecutor of her pagan rivals and of her own children. At length, stricken with a mortal sickness, Christ's vicegerent submits to receive Christ. The last act of Constantine is written in the cleansing water of baptism.

Who was Constantine, whom Christendom has alternately blessed and cursed? whose ambivalent gift to the Church was the double crown of thorns and gold? And what, in particular, has he to do with Colchester, that she should remember him in her Festival?

His father was Constantine Chlorus, appointed by Diocletian Augustus of the West, to rule the Provinces of Britain, Spain, and Gaul. His mother was that Helena who was later canonised as St. Helena, and whose finding of the True Cross in Jerusalem is commemorated in the Church's calendar on the third day of May. It was said by some, both then and now, that she was Constantine's concubine, a woman of humble origin—a barmaid, indeed, from Bithynia. But an ancient and respectable tradition affirms, on the other hand, that she was his lawful wife, a princess of Britain, daughter of the local chieftain "King" Coel of Colchester, whose legend, distorted by time, is preserved in the nursery song of "old King Cole". If this is so—and Colchester will hear no word to the contrary—she may well have been a Christian from her birth; for in the 4th century there was already a Christian church, with a Christian bishop, at Colchester. Her son may thus have received a bias towards Christianity from his early years; his father Constantius, though not a Christian, was a monotheist and favourably disposed to the Christians, steadily refusing to enforce the edicts of Diocletian against them. Constantine's own story, which he told to his biographer, Eusebius of Caesarea, is this. He said that one day, as he was riding across a plain in Gaul during his campaign against Maxentius, he saw a strange appearance round about the sun—the sign of the Chi-Ro, written in fire upon the sky; and that on the following night, in his tent, One came and showed him the sign again, saying to him: "*Hoc signo victor eris*: with this sign thou shalt be victor." And learning that the Chi and the Ro were the first letters of the name of Christ, he set the sign upon his shields, and the victory followed.

Thenceforth he was the elect servant of Christ. Yet we know that even before that time he was not indifferent to Christianity, for already among his most intimate counsellors he counted a Christian Bishop, the venerable Hosius of Cordova.

It seems possible to trace, running through the recorded acts, words, and writings of Constantine, a consistently developing apprehension of Christ. There is the Christ known to the pagan world, one god among many, worshipped by an increasingly numerous sect whose sober and disciplined life made it a valuable element in the State; there is Christ the Lord of Hosts, the powerful patron-deity of His Imperial Vicar; there is, later on, the Christ of the theologians, True God begotten of True God, the Holy and the One; there is, perhaps, in the end of all, Christ the Redeemer, sacrificed upon the wood of the Cross for the sins of man—and of Constantine. It is in this sense that the chronicle-play which we present at Colchester interprets the enigma of history.

The action of the play covers the twenty-one years from A.D. 305 to A.D. 326, with an Epilogue bringing the story to its close in the death of Constantine. The scene, moving without pause from Britain to Gaul, to Rome, to the Balkans, to Alexandria, to Byzantium, to Chrysopolis, to Nicaea, to Nicomedia, has no narrower limits than those of the Empire. The task of the playwright, crowding so much and such varied history into the short traffic of the stage, has been, if anything, rather less formidable than that of the producer and stage-designer, thus called upon to leap-frog a large cast of players across these vast expanses of space and time. The period, transitional between Late Classical and Early Byzantine, is one for which references are curiously scarce; here, as in the interpretation of character and motive, imagination must fill the gaps which the records do not supply.

The outline of the main events is, however, faithful to history and tradition, and the substance, if not the form, of the great theological argument which "split the Church for an iota" is that which was heard at Nicaea.

Of the two possible dates for the birth of Constantine I have, for dramatic convenience, chosen the later (see A. H. M. Jones, *Constantine and the Conversion of Europe*, pp. 1–2). The prayer issued for use by the army (Act I, Sc. 3) is historical, though connected with a later campaign. Historical, too, is Constantine's letter to the bishops in Act II, Sc. 7, as also his speech to the Council, and the letter from Arius to Eusebius of Nicomedia, in Act III, Sc. 5. The song sung by the Fishmonger's Boy in Act III, Scs. 2 and 3 is a (very) free adaptation from the *Thalia*—a popular poem composed by Arius and sung to "the tune of a bawdy song". That Fausta accused Crispus of attempted incest was alleged by the later historians to explain the double murder; but the suggestion that this accusation was part of a plot to dethrone Constantine is my own, and I have put back the date usually given for the execution of Licinius by a few months in order to tie up the ends of the plot more neatly. Similarly, to make the action more compact, I have caused Constantine to be baptized upon his death-bed, although in fact the ceremony took place a few days earlier, in a church near Nicomedia. The characters of Togius and Matibena have no historical foundation, neither has the prophecy spoken by Coel.

The text of the play is given as written; a number of cuts and modifications were made in production.

DRAMATIS PERSONAE

in the order of their appearance

THE CHURCH
COEL OF COLCHESTER
CABRUS
CARATILLUS } fiddlers attendant upon Coel
CARISSO
MATIBENA, a woman of Colchester, servant to Helena
TOGIUS ("TOGI"), a man of Colchester; afterwards secretary to Constantine
HELENA, daughter of Coel and mother to Constantine
FLAVIUS CONSTANTIUS CHLORUS, Augustus of the Western Empire, father to
  Constantine
CONSTANTINE
CAPTAIN
CENTURION } of the Army in Britain
COURIER
MAXIMIAN, formerly Augustus of the Western Empire
FAUSTA, his daughter; afterwards wife to Constantine
MARCUS
DECIUS
CAIUS } soldiers of the Army in Gaul
MANLIUS
PUBLIUS
CENTURION
ARMOURER } of the Army in Gaul
GENERAL SILVIUS
HOSIUS, Bishop of Cordova
CAPTAIN
LIVIA, wife to the Augustus Maxentius
TWO DAUGHTERS to Livia
MAJOR DOMO
AEMILIUS, an augur
CRASSUS, a senator
KNIGHT
ANNIUS ANULLINUS, Prefect of the City of Rome
OFFICER
MESSENGER
ZENOBIA
BERENICE
RHODA
PAULINA
THEODOSIA
CHLOE
DRUSILLA
FULVIA, a lady-in-waiting
LICINIUS, Augustus of the Eastern Empire
CONSTANTIA, wife to Licinius and sister to Constantine
CRISPUS CAESAR, son of Constantine by Minervina (at 12 years old)

9

CONSTANTINE CAESAR, son to Constantine by Fausta (at 3 years old)
LACTANTIUS, tutor to Crispus
BASSIANA MARCIA, attendant upon Fausta
HOST
POET
LAELIUS GALLUS, a rhapsodist
ALEXANDER, Bishop of Alexandria
ARIUS, a heresiarch
ATHANASIUS, a deacon of Alexandria
1ST SENTRY
2ND SENTRY
MESSENGER
CRISPUS CAESAR (at 19 years old)
EUSEBIUS, Bishop of Nicomedia
GENERAL ⎫
AUGUR ⎪
1ST SOOTHSAYER ⎬ attendant upon Licinius
2nd SOOTHSAYER ⎭
SPY
FISHMONGER'S BOY
PHILO ⎫
STEPHEN ⎬ barbers
EUTYCHUS ⎭
THEOPHILUS
DEACON JOHANNES, afterwards priest
PHILOSOPHER
GENTLEMAN
RETIRED GENERAL
BARBER'S BOY
JAMES, Bishop of Nisibis
THEOGNIS, Bishop of Nicaea
THEOPHILUS, Bishop of Pityontes
SPIRIDION, Bishop of Cyprus
EUSTATHIUS, Bishop of Antioch
AMPHION, Bishop of Epiphania
PAPHNUTIUS, Bishop of the Thebaid
PAUL, Bishop of Neocaesarea
EUSEBIUS, Bishop of Caesarea
POTAMON, Bishop of Heraclea
JOHN, Metropolitan of India
NICHOLAS, Bishop of Myra
SECUNDUS, Bishop of Ptolemais
MACARIUS, Bishop of Jerusalem
VINCENT ⎫
VICTOR ⎬ priests, representing the Bishop of Rome
THEONAS, Bishop of Marmarica
NICASIAS, Bishop of Die
SLAVE-GIRL
CRITO, a slave
CONSTANTINE CAESAR (at 12 years old)
Guards, Soldiers, Standard-Bearers, Lords, Ladies, Slaves and Attendants

THE EMPEROR CONSTANTINE

THE PROLOGUE

Enter the CHURCH, *habited in a white alb with a scarlet pall, having upon her head a crown of thorns and a crown of gold, and girded with a purse and a sword and bearing the Keys in her hand.*

CHURCH

Men and women of Christendom, I am your mother the Church. I was born in a poor fisherman's hut; but our Lord nourished and brought me up to be the Bride of the Trinity. While yet He sojourned in the world, He bade me learn the government of purse and sword, and made me keeper of the Keys of Heaven, by the hand of His servant Peter. His last gift to me was a crown of thorns; we shall show you now how His servant Constantine crowned me with a crown of gold. Sons and daughters, pray for the Church that she may come at last to be crowned with light in the courts of the Trinity.

ACT I

THE EMPIRE OF THE WEST

SCENE 1

A.D. 305—*King Coel's palace at Colchester.*

[*Before the rise of the Curtain, a distant trumpet. By the fire in a dim light,* COEL *asleep in his chair, with his three aged* FIDDLERS *sleeping beside him. Further down-stage* MATIBENA, *an elderly woman, spinning with a distaff by the light of a lamp.*

Trumpet again, nearer. MATIBENA *looks up for a moment and resumes her spinning. Enter* TOGI. *He looks round, does not see the person he wants and comes down to* MATIBENA.

MATIBENA

Was that a Roman trumpet?

TOGI (*agitated*)

More than Roman. Rome itself. Where is the Lady Helena?

MATIBENA

What do you mean, Rome? That old Prefect again?

TOGI

The Prefect? No. Augustus. (*He announces this as though it were the Last Trump.*)

MATIBENA (*unimpressed*)

What, him?

TOGI (*with a touch of sarcasm*)

Flavius Constantius Chlorus, Augustus of Britain, Gaul and Spain.

MATIBENA

Ah! he hadn't got all those handles to his name when he came here courting our young lady.

TOGI

Naturally not. That was twenty-two years ago. But he's Augustus now and he's here.

MATIBENA

Plain General Constantius was good enough for him when he wedded her. Till he cast her off, poor dear, with his nasty heathen

13

divorce, to marry the Emperor's niece and be called Caesar and Augustus.

TOGI

Obviously, it's all very awkward——

MATIBENA (*ignoring him*)

And taking her own son away from her to be brought up at that wicked foreign court where they persecute Christians and teach him to look down on us as common British savages as like as not.

TOGI (*desperately*)

Hadn't you better go and break it gently to the Lady Helena that her former husband——

MATIBENA

By God's law he's still her husband. And him Caesar of Britain these twelve years, skulking about at York and never so much as sending to say, "how are you". Ashamed of himself, I suppose, and well he may be, with our poor master never holding up his head again after his daughter was sent back to him like a cast-off cloak, but sits in a dream there by the fire all day, with those old fiddlers of his, him that was once merry King Coel of Colchester. If he was the man he used to be, he'd deal with General Constantius Chlorus, Augustus or no Augustus.

[*Trumpet just without.*

TOGI

There he is. Will you for Heaven's sake find the Lady Helena.

[*Enter* HELENA. *She is a gentle, dignified woman of about* 45, *with the remains of very great beauty.*

MATIBENA

If I were her I wouldn't let him in. I'd tell him to go and cool his heels in the Forum.

HELENA

Don't be ridiculous, Matibena. Of course we cannot refuse to receive Augustus.

MATIBENA

Oh, Madam dear, I was just coming to tell you——

14

HELENA

But you got talking treason instead; so I used my own eyes and ears. We will receive Augustus here. Togi, go to the kitchen, and tell them to lay supper in the private wing.

TOGI

At once, madam. (*He departs thankfully.*)

HELENA

Matibena, you will attend on me; and mind you behave yourself.

MATIBENA

Of course I shall attend on you. Who should, if it wasn't your old Matibena, that's nursed you and looked after you from the cradle? But oh, my lamb, I do say it's a wicked cruel shame——

HELENA

Never mind. (*Going towards* COEL) Father! . . . No, it would only trouble him. . . . We must be brave and sensible. Is my veil in order?

[MATIBENA *fusses about her. Noise of arrival, off.*

That will do. He's coming. (*She is a little overcome.*)

MATIBENA (*supporting her*)

There, there my pet, my precious. Don't give way. Look him straight in his wicked face till he blushes for it.

HELENA (*recovering herself, firmly*)

Stand behind me, please.

[*Enter* CONSTANTIUS CHLORUS, *attended by two* GUARDS.

GUARD

The Augustus Constantius.

[FLAVIUS CONSTANTIUS CHLORUS *is a care-worn, conscientious-looking man of about* 60, *who does not appear in the least villainous.* HELENA *allows him to walk the whole length of the room towards her, which in no way mitigates his embarrassment.*

15

Madam.

[HELENA *prostrates herself before him with the utmost ceremony,* MATIBENA *standing rigidly upright behind her with a grim scowl on her face.*

Madam, I beg of you.

[*It occurs to him that he would have done better to get rid of his* GUARDS *as soon as he got in. He is now obliged to turn and dismiss them, rather awkwardly, as they are at some distance behind him.*

(*To the Guards*) You may go.

[*The* GUARDS *withdraw.*

(*Extending his hand*) Helena, for pity's sake, don't kneel to me.

HELENA (*accepting his hand and rising*)

Not to you, Flavius, but to Augustus.

FLAVIUS

Is that irony?

HELENA

Just accuracy, Flavius. (*Formally*) You will forgive my father for not receiving you himself. He is a very old man, and his mind has become clouded of late.

FLAVIUS

I know. They told me. I am very sorry.

HELENA

You remember my old nurse, Matibena.

FLAVIUS

Indeed, yes.

MATIBENA (*compelled under* HELENA'S *eye, to some kind of reverence, which she executes as grudgingly as possible*)

I hope I see you well, sir. Though you don't look up to much. Your new lady doesn't take so much care of you as this one did. You'll excuse me not going down on my knees—they're too stiff, and I don't hold with these new foreign ways. They're all right for Eastern slaves, I've no doubt.

FLAVIUS (*preserving his dignity as best he can*)

We will excuse you.

HELENA

You hear, Matibena, Augustus will excuse you. So will I. Leave us, please. At once.

[MATIBENA *departs mutinously*.

I do apologise.

FLAVIUS

Poor old thing. You have hurt her feelings.

HELENA

She is very tiresome and devoted. But I cannot allow rudeness to Augustus—or to you, my dear.

FLAVIUS

Helena—if you know what a lout I feel——

HELENA

Oh, please. When we haven't met for ten years and have so much to say, don't let's waste time going over all that. I have never for one moment blamed you; it wasn't your fault, it was Diocletian's policy, you obeyed him with the greatest reluctance——

FLAVIUS

And I have never ceased to love you. (*He kisses her.*) Is that a sin in your Christian eyes?

HELENA

Not for me, because in my Christian eyes I am still your wife, though in Roman eyes you are Theodora's husband. Come and sit down and tell me about everything. . . . You haven't been unhappy, Flavius?

FLAVIUS

Not unhappy. No. Rather hard-worked. A little dull, perhaps. . . . (*Abruptly*) My youngest daughter is called Anastasia.

HELENA

Anastasia! That is a Christian name. It means "Resurrection".

17

FLAVIUS

You believe in a Resurrection where there will be no marriages—
and no divorces by Imperial command. I named her for that.

HELENA

May our Lord Christ bring you to His Resurrection. You are so
nearly a Christian, I am sure He will. And He will not forget that
you refused to persecute His people.

FLAVIUS

No, I did draw the line there. I don't know what came over
Diocletian. It's a very reactionary policy. But rulers get suspicious
as they grow older, and somebody must have put it in his head
that Christians were getting too numerous and might become
formidable.

HELENA

But that's absurd.

FLAVIUS

Not from his point of view. The Christians have discipline and
enthusiasm—pretty rare things in the Empire nowadays. Everybody's tired out and disillusioned, and now the old man's abdicated, I shouldn't wonder if the whole thing fell to pieces. It's
dying at the top. Rome's finished. The heart's taxed out of the
decent old native families, and this monstrous bureaucracy
chokes everything with red tape. Army discipline isn't what it was.
There's life in the provinces, but they'll break away some day.
One does what one can about education and so on—I've tried
my best, Helena.

HELENA

It's not like you to be so discouraged. Matibena is right; you're
not looking well, Flavius.

FLAVIUS

I've got something wrong with me. The doctors can't seem to do
anything, and I get so damnably tired. I don't think I shall last
much longer. That's why——There's one person you haven't
asked me about.

HELENA

Constantine. It was not for want of thinking about him. But I
wondered—Have you seen anything of him? I heard he was with
Diocletian.

FLAVIUS

Yes. The old man sent me west and kept the boy at court—as a hostage for my loyalty, I suppose. He trusts no one. But when Diocletian retired, I sent to Galerius—who has succeeded him, you know, as Augustus of the East——

HELENA

Yes, yes, I know.

FLAVIUS

—and told him I was ill, and should like to see my son—*our* son—again before I died.

HELENA

And he let him go?

FLAVIUS

He didn't much want to, but he did. Constantine joined me ten days ago at Boulogne.

HELENA

Oh, Flavius! You have seen him? Is he well? What is he like?

FLAVIUS

He is here.

HELENA

Here!

FLAVIUS

He was my excuse for coming. I thought, if you refused to see me, you would see him—that he might even persuade you to see me——

HELENA

Dear Flavius! How sweet you are, and how ridiculous! Is he in the palace? Can I see him now?

FLAVIUS

He is waiting to come in. (*He goes to the doorway.*)

HELENA

My little Constantine!

FLAVIUS (*shouting through the doorway*)

Captain!

19

VOICE (*off*)

Sir!

FLAVIUS

Inform the Lord Constantine that we wish to see him.

VOICE

Sir!

FLAVIUS (*starts to turn back, and then has a bright idea*)

And bring us some more lights!

VOICE (*a little further off*)

Sir!

HELENA

I haven't seen him since he was eleven. Shall I know him again?

FLAVIUS

He has grown a little in the last ten years. He is married now, with a little son of his own.

HELENA (*overwhelmed*)

Oh! . . . Oh, I can't wait! . . . But I'm glad we had those few moments alone together.

FLAVIUS (*moved*)

You are more gracious than I deserve.

GUARD

Lord Constantine.

[*Enter* CONSTANTINE, *attended by the two* GUARDS *carrying torches.*

[*The young man of* 21 *who thus breaks in upon this middle-aged idyll is very large, very tall, and good-looking in the rather heavy Roman fashion. Self-confidence is written in every line of his countenance. While* HELENA *composes herself to the dignity which, she feels, he will think becoming in a Roman matron, he sketches a duteous gesture towards his August father, and strides purposefully downstage towards her.*

FLAVIUS

My son, you remember your mother, the Princess Helena.

Indeed I do. (*He kneels at* HELENA's *feet with the rather clumsy grace of a handsome young cart-horse.*) Please give me your blessing, Mother.

CONSTANTINE

HELENA

God bless you, my dear boy. (*She sketches the sign of the cross almost imperceptibly upon his bent head.*) Stand up and let me see you.

[*He rises and she surveys him admiringly while the* GUARDS *place torches to illuminate that part of the stage and go out.*

What a great tall son I have!

CONSTANTINE (*gaily*)

And what a beautiful Mother I have. I always had. You haven't changed a bit.

HELENA

It's wonderful to see you, my dear. And I thought you were the width of the world away. Did you have a good journey?

CONSTANTINE

Well, it was rather exciting. Hasn't my father told you? (*He looks at* FLAVIUS *for permission to hold forth before his elders—he is well brought-up.* FLAVIUS *motions to him to go ahead, which he does.*) Old Galerius looked as sick as mud when Father's letter came. He didn't want to let me go, but he couldn't very well refuse his fellow-Augustus. So he took as long as he could to make out my passport, while I went round to a friend of mine—a very decent fellow who keeps a racing-stables—and made him sell me three of the fastest horses in Spalato. It was past midnight when my papers came through, but I'd made it right with the gate-keepers, and we got out—just me and a couple of stout lads I could trust—and we went hell-for-leather before anybody knew we'd started. Because of course I knew Galerius would have tipped off Severus and he'd try to stop me. He's Caesar of the West, you know, Mother, and of course he knows perfectly well that if it hadn't been for Diocletian's fads, I ought to have been Father's Caesar in the West, and I shall be some day, what's more.

FLAVIUS

My dear boy, we must respect Diocletian's arrangements.

21

CONSTANTINE

Yes, Father—but they won't work. . . . All the way to the first post we had our swords handy ready for anything. But they hadn't expected us to start before dawn, and we beat 'em to it. So we changed horses there, and my fellows went round and hamstrung every mount in the place, so they couldn't follow us. The post-master made a fearful hullabaloo, but I tipped him well and off we went again. You couldn't see us for dust. So we came all the way like that—eating and sleeping practically in the saddle, and killing the horses behind us, till we got to Boulogne more dead than alive, and so saddle-sore I went about bow-legged for a week. (*He laughs heartily at this recollection.*)

HELENA

My dear boy, I wonder you're alive to tell the tale. Was it really necessary to be so—ruthless?

FLAVIUS

He showed great foresight and resolution, Helena. I've no doubt they'd have stopped him if they could.

CONSTANTINE

It cost a bit of money. I had to go to the usurers. But I told them I'd pay it all back with interest when I was Emperor.

FLAVIUS

By Diocletian's wishes, the sons of the Augusti are expressly excluded from succeeding to the purple.

CONSTANTINE

Quite so, sir. But I shall be Emperor one day for all that. Not for a very long time, I hope. But the Army won't want anybody but me to come after you.

FLAVIUS (*annoyed*)

Constantine——

HELENA

There now! You look just as you were at six years old—shouting "I'm King of the Castle" and never letting the other boys have their turn. You remember, in our old garden in Nyssa?

22

[*Whether this is maternal tactlessness or maternal guile, it has the effect of momentarily deflating* CONSTANTINE *and distracting his father's attention.*

FLAVIUS

We had very happy times at Nyssa.

HELENA

And at Drepanum, when we were first married.

FLAVIUS

And were billeted at that big inn with the farmyard, and the pigs *would* always wander into the dining-room.

HELENA

And the day the landlady was taken ill, when I went and gave them a hand in the bar. And you were so cross with that fat wool-merchant who wanted me to sit on his knee.

FLAVIUS

You wouldn't have liked it if I *hadn't* been cross. Actually I had every sympathy with the man.

CONSTANTINE

So *that's* why!

FLAVIUS

Why what?

HELENA

What's why, darling?

CONSTANTINE

That's why they call me the barmaid's bastard.

FLAVIUS

Do they, by God!

HELENA (*conscience-stricken*)

My dearest boy! How dreadful! Somebody must have recognised me and thought—Oh, dear, I'm so sorry——

Don't worry, Mother. I didn't contradict them. (*Grimly*) It's been safer these last few years to be the by-blow of a Bithynian barmaid than the son of a Christian princess.

FLAVIUS

That's true enough.

CONSTANTINE

By the way, since the subject has cropped up—do you mind telling me whether I am legitimate or not? Just as a matter of curiosity.

FLAVIUS

It's a little complicated. Your mother and I were married here in Colchester by the Christian bishop. I'm not sure what attitude Rome takes about that. But when you were born at Nyssa, I recognised you in the Roman way as my rightful son. Then when Diocletian insisted on my marrying your step-mother, I was obliged to divorce your mother, by Roman law. But Christians don't recognise our State divorces, so you see——

CONSTANTINE

So in Christian eyes, you two are still married?

HELENA

Yes.

CONSTANTINE (*to* FLAVIUS)

And I'm not merely legitimate, but your *only* legitimate son?

FLAVIUS

In Christian eyes, yes.

CONSTANTINE

I see. I'll remember that. I owe Christ something. Is He a strong god?

HELENA

He is the one true God. Have you forgotten what I taught you about Him?

CONSTANTINE

There are so many gods in the Empire, Mother. We praise the official gods on public holidays and cultivate a more spiritual attitude to life in our spare time. It's all rather decadent and disintegrating. The Empire needs pulling together—a new focus of faith and energy. What do you think, Father?

FLAVIUS (*with a faint smile*)

In my position as Pontifex Maximus, I can't afford to be original. I have to perform the official rites and honour the customary deities. But I think they are all types and shadows of the One God, and I believe in Him.

[*Here* COEL, *who has been stirring in his sleep during the last few minutes, draws his hand across the strings of his harp. They turn, startled.*

CONSTANTINE

What's that? (*He notices* COEL *for the first time.*) Why, Mother, who is this magnificent old man?

HELENA

King Coel of Colchester. Your grandfather.

CONSTANTINE

You never told me. I ought to have paid my respects to him.

HELENA

He is very old. Once he was a great chieftain and a great harper, and had the gift of prophecy. But now, all his life has become a sleep beside the fire. I am afraid you will not rouse him.

CONSTANTINE

One could try, at least. May I try? (*Without waiting for permission, he goes up to* COEL.) Grandfather! Can you hear me? Won't you look at me? (*He kicks the logs apart, so that the fire flares up.*) See! (*He kneels before him.*) Speak to me, Coel of Colchester; I am your grandson Constantine.

COEL

Constantine. (*He stares into the young man's face.*)

CONSTANTINE

Son of your daughter Helena and the Emperor Constantius Chlorus.

CoEL

I know you, child, I know you. Constantine the Roman. Son of the old Rome, father of the New. I have seen your face in my dreams. (*He lifts his hand and speaks in a stronger voice.*) Cabrus, Caratillus, Carisso! Bring me my rod and my bowl, for the Powers that stand at his shoulder are Time and Change and Fortune. Be merry, my fiddlers, tune your crowds; play for the last weird of Coel of Camulodunum.

[*The Three* FIDDLERS *creep from their places and gather about him. One of them gives him a brazen bowl and a rod of divination, and takes up* COEL'S *harp. The other two have ancient viols. They pluck the strings softly.*

CONSTANTINE

Coel of Camulodunum, what do you know of Constantine?

COEL (*setting the bowl in* CONSTANTINE'S *hands and laying the rod upon his head*)

Look in the bowl; look well, and tell me what you see.

CONSTANTINE

Nothing. Mist and darkness. I am a doer, I think, not a seer.

COEL

Well said, for so you are. But I see the golden sickle thrust in among the branches, and the leaves falling from all the trees of the world.

CONSTANTINE

Speak. I am here. I am listening. I am Constantine.

[COEL *rises to his feet; the* FIDDLERS *play.*

COEL (*speaking over the music*)

Coel the son of Coel the son of Coel the heaven-born;
I have harped in the Twelve Houses; I have prophesied among
the Dancers;
Coel, father of the Light, who bears the Sun in her bosom.

Three times have I seen the Cross:
Air and fire in Gaul, under the earth in Jerusalem,
Written upon water in the place of the victories.

Three times have I heard the Word:
The word in a dream, and the word in council,
The word of the Word within the courts of the Trinity.

Three Crowns: laurel among the trumpets,
A diadem of stars with fillets of purple,
Thorns and gold for the Bride of the Trinity.

I have seen Constantine in the air as a flying eagle,
I have seen Constantine in the earth as a raging lion,
I have seen Constantine in the water as a swimming fish.

Earth and water and air—but the beginning and the ending is
fire,
Light in the first day, fire in the last day, at the coming of the
Word,
And Our Lord the Spirit descending in light and in fire.

[*The rod drops from his hand, and he sinks back into the arms of the*
FIDDLERS, *two of whom help him back to his chair, while the third takes
the bowl from* CONSTANTINE.

CONSTANTINE (*leaping to his feet*)

The eagles! the eagles! Did you hear that? (*He strides exultantly
down to his parents, who are too stunned to say anything.*) Did you hear
him promise me the diadem and the purple? Did I not tell you I
should be Emperor? Your prophecy shall come true, Coel of
Camulodunum—I'll see to it, never you fear. (*A thought strikes him
and he goes back to* COEL.) Why did you speak of the cross? (*But
COEL has returned to his dreams.*) Never mind. We shall know some
day. (*He is still puzzled.*) "A flying eagle, a raging lion . . . a
swimming fish." Mother, why did he call me a fish? (*Laughing*)
Do I look like a fish? It doesn't matter. Wife of an Emperor,
Mother of Emperors, you shall be Empress of Old and New Rome.
. . . And talking of fish, will there be oysters for supper?

SCENE 2

A.D. 306—YORK. (*Before tabs.*)

[*Enter R. a* GUARDS CAPTAIN *with a* CENTURION *carrying a purple
cloak and a gold laurel-chaplet.*

27

CAPTAIN

Now, Centurion, you know what you have to do? Are the men prepared?

CENTURION

Yessir.

CAPTAIN

You and the rest of the deputation come forward and stand behind me while I speak my piece. Then he has to pretend to refuse. Then I say the Army won't take no for an answer and the men get the signal to shout. Who's doing that?

CENTURION

Standard-bearer, sir.

CAPTAIN

Good. Then he says that what the Army says goes: then you step up smartly with the purple and we put it on him, the men carry him out and everybody cheers. Got that?

CENTURION

Yessir.

CAPTAIN

Right. Go and wait till I'm ready for you, and see that they all know their stuff.

[*The* CENTURION *goes out R. Enter L.* TOGI, *and a* COURIER *carrying a parcel wrapped up in a cloth.*

Is the Lord Constantine ready to receive the deputation from the Army?

COURIER

He is coming; but he asks you to excuse him for a moment while he gives us our instructions. He has letters to send.

CAPTAIN

Very well. (*He steps back R. out of sight.*)

COURIER (*to* TOGI)

You ride to Colchester?

TOGI

Yes. I must take this sad news to Lord Constantine's mother. She will be deeply grieved, poor lady.

I'm for Rome. And I fancy the Emperor Galerius won't much like the news either, if *this* is anything to go by. (*He taps the parcel.*)

TOGI

What is it?

COURIER

Just a little present from York.

[*Enter* CONSTANTINE *L. bareheaded in a mourning garment, carrying letters.*

CONSTANTINE

The Lady Helena's servant?

[TOGI *steps forward.*

Ah, yes. What's your name?

TOGI

Togius, sir. They call me Togi.

CONSTANTINE

Of course, I remember you. I saw you last year at Colchester. You asked if you might take service with me. What can you do?

TOGI

Ride a horse, swim a river, throw a spear. Read Latin and Greek, write a good clear hand, obey orders and keep my temper.

CONSTANTINE

I might find a use for you. But now, take this letter to your mistress. Give her my most dutiful love. Tell her that my father's last words were "Helena" and "Resurrection".

TOGI

I will, sir. (*Going.*)

CONSTANTINE

Wait a moment. You may have other news to carry. (*He beckons the* COURIER.) Have you got the portrait?

COURIER

Here it is. (*He opens the parcel and displays a bust.*)

CONSTANTINE (*examining it*)

Is it like me?

COURIER

It doesn't do you justice. But in case the Augustus can't recognise it, your name is carved on the base.

CONSTANTINE (*producing a small bay-wreath from under his garment and crowning the bust with it*)

That will improve its appearance. Wait here. In certain circumstances, which you will easily recognise, you will carry it, bay-wreath and all, to his Augustitude in Rome, and give it to him with this letter. And you will ride like hell.

COURIER (*appreciatively*)

Like hell, sir.

CONSTANTINE

In which case, Togius, you will return to my mother, tell her what has happened, and wait in Colchester till I send word to her to join me in Gaul. If, on the other hand, the circumstances should fail to arise, I will give you (*to the* COURIER) another letter, which you can convey at your leisure.

COURIER

With no portrait?

CONSTANTINE

And no bays. And in that case, *you* (*to* TOGI) can just go quietly home. . . . Now then. I think there are some Army officers waiting to see me.

COURIER

Yes, sir.

[*The* COURIER *beckons to the* CAPTAIN, *who enters, followed by* CENTURION, STANDARD-BEARER *and* SOLDIERS. COURIER *and* TOGI *retire L. but stand within hearing.*

(*To* TOGI *as they move away*) The situation appears to be well in hand.

[TOGI, *who has not yet grasped what the situation is, tries to look as though he knows all about it.*)

CONSTANTINE

Well, Captain, what is it?

CAPTAIN

Sir. The Army of Britain desire to convey to you their respectful sympathy upon the death of your honoured father, the Augustus Constantius. He was a good Emperor, sir, and a fine general, and all the men are very sorry to lose him.

CONSTANTINE

Thank you, Captain. Tell them, I am greatly touched by their kind message. My August father would have valued this tribute. His heart was always very much with the Army.

CAPTAIN

Yes, sir. Thank you, sir. Further, sir, the Army desire to remind you that it is their privilege to choose the new Augustus in succession to your father, and, in short, sir, to say that they have chosen you.

CONSTANTINE (*modestly*)

Captain, I am greatly honoured, I am deeply obliged. But indeed I am not worthy. I am young and inexperienced. There are many better and more deserving candidates.

CAPTAIN

You are the right man for us, sir.

CONSTANTINE

I believe the Emperor Galerius has other plans——

CAPTAIN

Excuse me, sir, but nobody's going to do us out of our lawful rights.

[*The rest of the* DEPUTATION *back this up with a helpful growl.*

The Army want you, sir, and they won't take no for an answer.

[*Here the* STANDARD-BEARER, *recognising his cue, lifts up the standard, and is rewarded by a gratifying outburst from the* ARMY, *off R.*

ARMY (*off R.*)

Constantine! Constantine for Augustus! Imperator Constantinus! Constantine for Emperor! Give us Constantine! Constantine for ever! (*And other such sentiments.*)

CAPTAIN

Hear that, sir? What about it? The lads are getting impatient.

[*Everything is going according to plan.*

CONSTANTINE (*with a gesture of surrender*)

I am in your hands. If it is the will of the Army——

CAPTAIN (*to the* DEPUTATION)

He consents.

[*The* CENTURION *rushes up with the cloak.*

STANDARD-BEARER (*in a stentorian yell to the* ARMY)

He consents! Long live the Emperor Constantine!

[*A tremendous roar goes up. The* DEPUTATION *put the purple and the chaplet on* CONSTANTINE *and hoist him shoulder-high.*

CONSTANTINE (*to the* COURIER)

To Rome, and burn the road!

[COURIER *waves the bust with its bay-wreath exultantly, and dashes out L.*

(*To* TOGI) Tell my Mother! Tell Colchester! Tell Britain!

[TOGI, *now enlightened, gives a Roman salute and follows* COURIER *off.*

TOGI and COURIER (*shouting off L.*)

Horses! Horses!

[*The cheers redouble as* CONSTANTINE *is borne off R.*

SCENE 3

February 307—GAUL: *a room in a palace.* ($\frac{1}{2}$ *set A.*)

[HELENA *discovered reading. She follows the lines with her finger, making lip-movements as she goes along. Presently she finishes her portion for the day, lays the book open in her lap, and prays silently.* MATIBENA *looks in, with a breakfast-tray, and hovers till* HELENA *crosses herself and opens her eyes.*

MATIBENA

Finished saying your prayers?

Yes, thank you.

[MATIBENA *puts the tray beside her.*

Well, Matibena, what do you think of life in Gaul?

Much the same as life anywhere else. Only you can't get any fresh fish. (*She gathers up the book.*) This what the bishop gave you? I like the pictures. But all those nasty black marks look more like magic to me. I can say my prayers without any book.

They will reach God quite as quickly. I hope you remember to pray for the soul of the King my Father.

Yes, of course. But he doesn't need prayers from a wicked old woman like me. He's gone straight to Heaven.

And that the Lord Constantine may become a servant of Christ?

I wouldn't presume to put it that way. "Servant", indeed. He wants the top seat, like the blessed disciples at the Lord's supper. You'd better read him that bit. Do young Togi good, too. There's no holding him, now he's been made secretary to Constantine Augustus.

To Constantine Caesar.

Oh? I thought they'd made him Augustus up in York.

The British Army did. But the Augustus Galerius wouldn't agree. He made Severus Augustus of the West and said Lord Constantine must be content with the title of Caesar.

He won't be content long, if I know him. . . . That kitten's been at your basket again. . . . Who's the old gentleman who arrived last night? He had himself announced as Augustus.

HELENA

So he is, in a way. He's Maximian, who used to be the Western
Augustus when Diocletian was Augustus in the East. He abdicated when Diocletian did. But last year his son Maxentius
rebelled against Severus and took the purple from him and set
himself up as Augustus. And then he brought his father back to
Rome and made *him* Augustus too.

MATIBENA (*busy with* HELENA's *spools of silks*)

That's four of them calling themselves Augustus. There's Galerius
—he's tip-top emperor of the lot, isn't he?

HELENA

Yes—he's Senior Augustus and governs the Eastern Empire.

MATIBENA

And the one who was beaten in the rebellion.

HELENA

Severus—but I rather think——

MATIBENA

And this old Maximian and his son what's-his-name.

HELENA

Maxentius—those are the two in Rome.

MATIBENA

Not counting our Constantine, who ought to be Augustus and
isn't. Too many cooks, if you ask me.

HELENA

In Diocletian's time there was a Senior Augustus in the East and
a Junior Augustus in the West, and they each had a Caesar as a
kind of assistant-emperor.

MATIBENA

And now everybody's too grand to be Caesar and wants to be a
proper emperor. . . . Is there a Caesar in the East?

34

HELENA

Yes—a man called Maximin—a cruel man and a persecutor.

MATIBENA

Another Max! You'd think they did it on purpose to muddle you!
. . . Maximin . . . he assists Galerius I suppose. And Constantine's
Caesar of the West. Who's he assisting?

HELENA

Really, Matibena, I don't quite know. But I think Maximian has
come to ask for his alliance. If he gets it, he'll probably have to
let Constantine have the title of Augustus.

MATIBENA

That'll make five of them. But I expect they'll kill off the ones
they don't want.

HELENA

I rather think they *have* killed off Severus.

MATIBENA

I shouldn't be surprised. . . . That one's empty; the kitten can
have it. (*She throws the empty spool aside.*) . . . Who's the young lady
that came with the Augustus-or-whatever-he-is Maximian?

HELENA

That's his daughter, the Lady Fausta.

MATIBENA

What's *she* after?

HELENA

I couldn't tell you.

MATIBENA

Meaning it's not my business. But I can guess all right. And what
I say is, the Lord Constantine is a married man with a son of his
own, and if I were you, I wouldn't countenance anything of the
sort, not after what you've been through, and history repeating
itself as you might say——

[TOGI *has entered and is hesitating at the door.*

35

HELENA

That will do, Matibena. I think Togi wants to see me. Ask him to come in.

MATIBENA (*to* TOGI)

Her ladyship desires the Lord High Secretary to be good enough to step this way.

TOGI (*giving* MATIBENA *a withering look, which only amuses her*)

Madam.

[HELENA *signs to him to proceed.*

Constantine Caesar's duty and compliments, and he begs that you will oblige him by receiving the Lady Fausta while he and the Augustus Maximian are in conference.

HELENA

Certainly, with pleasure.

TOGI

Er—excuse me, madam, but I would suggest with all respect that it might be well to put any Christian books or emblems out of sight for the moment. Although the Augustus is very liberal minded, the Edicts are still technically in force, and if the young lady were to notice anything——

MATIBENA (*snatching up the book and putting it on the tray under a napkin*)

You mean she's a spy. Will that do? Quite the little politician, aren't you? No mind at all to be a Christian martyr! And take that smirk off your face.

TOGI

The truth is, madam, that we have rather a ticklish interview in front of us——

MATIBENA

We! us!

TOGI

—and Caesar is anxious that any stipulations he may wish to make in the matter of religious toleration should not appear to be dictated by personal considerations. (*Suddenly abandoning his official manner*) Oh, madam, everything's going to be all right. Take my word for it. The most terrifically exciting things are going to happen. (*Recovering it*) Caesar further requests, madam, that in about half an hour's time, you will walk alone in the hall.

Very well, Togi; I quite understand. Matibena, take these things away, and tell the Lady Fausta that I shall be delighted to have her company.

[*Exit* MATIBENA *with the tray.*]

Togi, you are getting quite a taste of high politics. I am glad my son has given you the opportunity. But don't let it go to your head.

TOGI

No, madam.

HELENA

It's exciting, but it can be heart-breaking. You may see things that will shock you. Constantine is set on the road to power, and power is a great responsibility. No one who does not share the responsibility has any right to judge. Our Lord said, Do not judge.

TOGI

I'll remember that, madam.

HELENA

I don't want to be discouraging. Forgive me. . . . Here come our guests.

[MATIBENA *returns with* MAXIMIAN, *a stout, hearty man of* 60 *or so, and* FAUSTA, *a handsome, temperamental-looking girl of about* 17. HELENA *receives* MAXIMIAN *with courtesy, but as no more than an equal.*]

Good morning, my Lord Maximian; good morning, dear Fausta. I hope you slept well.

MAXIMIAN

Excellently, dear lady, excellently. February Fill-dyke, eh? always a cold month in Gaul, but your house is admirably heated. I've brought my little girl along to see you while Constantine and I talk politics. You'll find her well-brought-up, though I say it. She's a real little housekeeper to me, since her dear mother died and her sisters married. She's brought her bit of sewing along—always busy, aren't you, puss? . . . She's rather young to be running about the world like this, but things aren't too settled in Rome, and I thought she'd be safer with her old dad.

37

We are very glad to see her.

[TOGI *goes through curtain to ½ set B.*

MAXIMIAN

Yes, yes. She and Constantine were great friends, you know, in the old days—regular little sweethearts. Don't blush, poppet—you were only about so high. We've a charming picture of 'em in our place at Aquileia—family group, you know. Your boy in his little suit of armour, done to the life, and Fausta bringing him his helmet—almost as big as herself—toddling along with it in her little plump arms—Mars and Venus in the nursery, ha, ha!

FAUSTA

Father, please!

MAXIMIAN

Everybody who sees it, says, "How sweet!"

[TOGI *emerges again and stands holding back the curtain*

HELENA (*with almost imperceptible irony*)

I'm sure they do.

MAXIMIAN

Yes; indeed, especially the ladies. (*To* TOGI) Well, young man, is your master ready for me?

TOGI

Caesar is waiting to receive you, sir.

[MAXIMIAN *goes in B.*

HELENA

Come along, my dear, this is my sitting-room. You will find it nice and sunny. (*They go in A.*) Draw the curtain, Matibena; there is a draught from the hall.

[*Curtain drawn on ½ set A.*

[*Meanwhile,* CONSTANTINE *is disclosed—½ set B—in his study, rather ostentatiously immersed in official correspondence. He looks up with a nicely calculated start.*

CONSTANTINE

Ah! at your service, sir. Togi, a seat for the Lord Maximian. You don't mind my secretary being present. We might want a few notes taken.

Quite right. Best to be methodical. Always Diocletian's way. Great man, Diocletian. Managed to reign twenty years and keep a whole skin. . . . Well, now. You know something about the situation in Rome.

CONSTANTINE (*lightly indicating a basket bulging with reports*)
We are fairly well informed.

MAXIMIAN

That fellow Severus was no good at all. Had to eliminate him. Riots in the city. Troops disaffected. Diocletian's idea, putting in all these new men—great statesmen, but a bit of an idealist. Always told him it was a mistake for both of us to abdicate. Should have let me carry on. Soldiers want somebody they know and trust.

CONSTANTINE

Very true, sir. The confidence I enjoy in my own province is wholly due td the people's loyal affection for my late father's memory.

MAXIMIAN

Quite, quite. The British wanted you for Augustus, didn't they?
[CONSTANTINE *bows.*
Honest fellows! A little premature, but very gratifying. Britain's a one-horse place, but every little helps. Spain didn't recognise you?

CONSTANTINE

My father was not personally known in Spain.

MAXIMIAN

No, no. Spain and Africa are all for *my* boy, of course. They haven't forgotten their old Augustus. So that, with Maxentius and me in Rome, and you as Caesar of Gaul and Britain, we control the whole West.

CONSTANTINE

Just a moment, sir. Galerius has already recognised me as Caesar——

MAXIMIAN

Reluctantly.

39

Reluctantly, if you like. But he has. And seeing that he is now advancing in force upon Maxentius——

You needn't worry about that. His troops will come over to us. And between you and me, my dear lad, if I were to set up my standard in Gaul——

CONSTANTINE

My troops would do the same? If you think that, why come to me?

MAXIMIAN

Because, bless my heart, I'd much rather do things in a friendly way. You're young and ambitious—quite right, I like you for it —and I'd be glad to do you a good turn.

CONSTANTINE

Very good of you, sir.

MAXIMIAN

Now, if you come in with us, we've got the whole thing on a plate.

CONSTANTINE

Whereas, if I choose to be awkward, Maxentius will be cracked like a nut between Galerius on one side and me on the other before your Spanish and African reinforcements can take Marseilles or cross the Pyrenees.

MAXIMIAN

Now, now, I can't admit that.

CONSTANTINE

Then we'll take it as read. If, on the other hand, I do come in with you—and it would have to be on equal terms, as Augustus——

MAXIMIAN

By all means. We shan't quarrel about that.

CONSTANTINE

I shall be taking a big risk. And for what? For a title which I shall get from Galerius if I wait long enough. And I shall have put myself in a false position by taking up arms against the lawful Augustus. Not good enough.

MAXIMIAN

You're too hasty. I haven't asked you to take up arms.

CONSTANTINE

I see. You want me to keep Gaul and Britain out of the ring while Maxentius fights it out with Galerius.

MAXIMIAN

If that's all you're willing to do. At your age, I should have had more spirit.

CONSTANTINE

If you had been brought up like me, Maximian, you would have learnt caution. The first lesson I got by heart was to hold my tongue and trust nobody. Supposing I do what you want—what security can you give me?

MAXIMIAN

Fausta.

CONSTANTINE

Fausta?

MAXIMIAN

Marry her. Be son to me and brother to Maxentius. Make the Empire a family affair.

CONSTANTINE

You forget that I am married already. Minervina is a good wife and fruitful. She has done nothing to deserve divorce.

MAXIMIAN

No, no, indeed. But your marriage was only a political arrangement forced on you both by Diocletian.

CONSTANTINE

In order to prevent precisely the alliance you are now suggesting.

MAXIMIAN

Just so. You and Fausta were practically affianced from the cradle. But Diocletian thought it would make you and your father too powerful. Dear, dear—poor Diocletian, a wonderful man but suspicious of everybody. Such a pity! But if he wanted to go on dictating world-policy, he shouldn't have abdicated. Now you've got your opportunity, take it and use it. Fausta's a pretty girl, and a good girl. Fond of you, too. And your sons would be grandchildren of emperors on both sides.

CONSTANTINE

Do you expect me to disinherit my eldest son? Or leave him as a hostage in the East, as my father had to leave me? I'll not do that. Crispus stays with me, whatever happens.

MAXIMIAN

Well, well. Time enough to discuss that when he's older. Come now, Constantine, make up your mind. Will you stand with us? Or rely on the favour of Galerius, who doesn't like you and may revoke your powers at any moment, or put in some other incompetent like Severus, to be Augustus over your head?

CONSTANTINE

Or like Maximin Daia, who's another religious maniac like himself, and spends all his time persecuting Christians and inventing tests of loyalty. I hope, by the way, Maxentius will keep off that. My father was always for toleration and letting well alone.

MAXIMIAN

My dear boy, I couldn't agree with you more. These tests don't mean a thing. Tell you the truth, when I see a man sacrificing to my deity, it makes me nervous. He might think it his duty to send me to join the gods next day, in token of his sincerity, ha, ha! Good behaviour's the best test of loyalty, and I've always found these Christians orderly and obedient in all practical matters.

CONSTANTINE

Yes. It seems they don't believe in violence and rebellion. I had a very sensible letter the other day from some bishop or other in Spain——

MAXIMIAN (startled)

In Spain?

42

CONSTANTINE

Oh, yes. I have some connections in Spain. . . . No, Togi, no—
the name doesn't matter. . . . He spoke of my father with very
touching appreciation.

MAXIMIAN

Well, we shan't interfere with him.

[HELENA *comes out and walks in the hall.*

CONSTANTINE

I thought I'd just mention it, that's all. . . . Excuse me, I think my
Mother wants to speak to me. . . . Togi, just jot down those
various points for the Lord Maximian to consider. (*He comes out
and joins* HELENA.) Well, Mother?

HELENA

Well, my son. Have you got what you wanted?

CONSTANTINE

Easily. Too easily. If the old man was sure of himself he'd have
driven a harder bargain. And I don't trust that blighter Maxentius
a yard. Still—Maximian's name counts for a lot at the moment,
and I think it's worth it.

HELENA

Your first exercise in diplomacy.

CONSTANTINE

It hasn't gone too badly. I've more or less agreed to the marriage.
. . . Don't worry, Mother. It won't upset Minervina, and I've kept
control over Crispus. . . . Do you approve of Fausta?

HELENA

She will play the part of Augusta very well. But be careful. She
is a proud, passionate girl—and in love with you.

CONSTANTINE

Is she? All the better—it should keep her faithful. . . . That
ought to please you, Mother. You like a love-match. Well,
fetch her along and let's get things settled. (*Hailing* MAXIMIAN)
Are the terms all right, sir?

MAXIMIAN

I'm satisfied, if you are.

CONSTANTINE

Read them out, Togi.

TOGI

The Lord Constantine undertakes to acknowledge the Lords Maximian and Maxentius as joint Augusti in Italy, Spain, and Africa and to observe a friendly neutrality in Gaul and Britain while they establish their claims with the Emperor Galerius. Further, he undertakes to divorce his present wife, the Lady Minervina, but without prejudice to the rights of his son Crispus by that lady. In return, the Lords Maximian and Maxentius undertake to acknowledge the Lord Constantine as Augustus on equal terms with themselves, and with full jurisdiction over the provinces of Gaul and Britain. Further, to give him the hand of the Lady Fausta in marriage—er—I have tentatively added "with a suitable dowry"?

MAXIMIAN

Yes; yes. We will go into that after dinner.

TOGI

With a suitable dowry, and to exercise religious toleration to all Christians—

CONSTANTINE

Better make it general.

TOGI

To exercise religious toleration throughout the Western Empire.

MAXIMIAN

That's everything, I think.

CONSTANTINE (*politely*)

Except the consent of the lady.

MAXIMIAN

Oh, ah, to be sure. The modern young woman likes to be consulted, eh? What do you say, my dear? Have you any objection to this great lad here?

FAUSTA

I am willing to obey you in everything, Papa.

MAXIMIAN

Good girl.

CONSTANTINE

Will you marry me, Fausta?

FAUSTA

Gladly, Constantine—if we have your mother's consent.

HELENA

You have my consent.

MAXIMIAN

Very good, then, Augustus—we are agreed.

CONSTANTINE

We are agreed, Augustus.

[*They shake hands on it.*

HELENA

Come into the state-parlour. We must have a cup of wine to celebrate the event.

[*Exit with* MAXIMIAN *and* FAUSTA.

MATIBENA (*following them off*)

A nice morning's work, I must say.

CONSTANTINE

Togi. What was the name of that Spanish bishop?

TOGI

Hosius, Bishop of Cordova.

CONSTANTINE

Come to my study in an hour's time. We will invite him to pay us a visit.

[*Exeunt* CONSTANTINE *and* TOGI *behind the rest of the party.*

SCENE 4

MARCUS

Nah! you got it all wrong. Jest you listen. This 'ere Maxentius, wot we're fighting against, 'e made 'isself emperor five years back, see? And 'e dug out 'is old pop, Maximian, and made 'im emperor too, and sent 'im to fix up an alliance with our Constantine, and marry off 'is daughter Fausta to 'im, wot's this Maxentius's sister. Got that? Which the old boy done. So then Maxentius says to his dad, " Dad ", 'e says, " you done your stuff and I ain't got no more use for you ", see?

DECIUS

Dirty dog!

MARCUS

So old Maximian starts cussin' and swearin' and tries to 'ave the purple off 'im, see? But the troops only laughs at 'im, and the old boy runs off to Constantine, 'owling blue murder. And Constantine treats 'im very kind, but 'e don't give 'im no power, see? because of upsettin' Maxentius. Besides, the old boy was past it. But any'ow, Maxentius 'ad 'is 'ands full, because Africa goes and 'as a rebellion and sets up a new Augustus on its own.

CAIUS

Was that the year we had six emperors at once?

MARCUS

That's right. Old Diocletian, he comes and sticks 'is finger in the pie, and appoints another new Augustus—Licinius, that was—and then Constantine and Maximin Daia they got on their 'ind legs and said they'd got to be Augustus too, and there was a rare old muddle.

MANLIUS

But what 'appened to Maximian? . . . Shove that paint pot over.

MARCUS

Well, 'e waits till Constantine's tied up with fightin' the Germans, and then 'e stages what they call a coop.

46

CAIUS

Coop?

MARCUS

Ah! that's Greek for a big bust-up. 'E gives out as Constantine's been killed——

PUBLIUS

That's right. I knows all about that——

MARCUS

—and proclaims 'isself Augustus of Gaul—in Arles, that was—and 'e calls on the troops there to lend 'im a 'and. But Constantine gets wind of it at Cologne, and comes back 'ell-for-leather——

PUBLIUS

That's right. I was in that. Coo! that was a do, that was. We was that mad keen, we couldn't wait, not even for supplies. We legged it by forced marches to Châlons and then down the Rhone in them mucky old barges—sweatin' at the oars like a bunch of galley-slaves, they were that damn slow—all the way to Marseilles. Old Maximian bolted there like a rabbit, and he thought 'e was all right, because our ladders was too short for the walls. But when the boys inside see we'd got Constantine with us, they opened the gates. A fair picnic it was, and no mistake.

CAIUS

Ay, Constantine can move. Come to think on't we've done none too bad this trip, comin' over the Alps an' all. And Turin—that wasn't no picnic. When I see all that 'eavy cavalry a-makin' for us, " Caius, my lad ", I says to myself, " Your number's up for sure ", I says——

DECIUS

Ah! but Constantine took their measure proper. " Let 'em coom, lads ", 'e says, " let 'em coom "——

MANLIUS

All right, all right, we've all been there. But what 'appened to Maximian?

MARCUS

I'm telling you, ain't I? Constantine acted very decent, and spared 'is life, seein' 'e was 'is father-in-law and all that. But

Maximian, 'e says to 'is daughter, " Fausta, my girl ", 'e says,
" leave your bedroom door ajar an' I'll slip in an' slit the throat
of that son of a bitch of a 'usband of yours ", he says.

PUBLIUS

Must a-bin barmy, the silly old coot.

MARCUS

But she was a good girl, you see, and went an' told her hubby,
and they fixed up to put a low-down slave in Constantine's bed
that night——

DECIUS

Nice for the slave.

MARCUS

Ah, he weren't no good—barbarian trash, and drunk as a
fiddler's bitch, anyhow. . . . So in goes old Maximian with a
long knife and bungs it into 'im, plonk! And then Constantine
comes along with the guard——

DECIUS

Some story. (*He spits contemptuously.*)

MARCUS

Fact. I oughter know. I was in the palace meself, and my mate
Rufus was the one as took 'im. So Constantine spares 'is life
again and shoves 'im in quod, and the old blighter 'angs 'imself
out o' re-morse.

DECIUS

So *they* say.

MARCUS

Wotcher mean, *they* say?

DECIUS

That's the official dope they dish out. But if you ask me, they
done the old man in and thought that tale up to save their faces.

MARCUS

Now, see 'ere!

PUBLIUS

Steady on, there!

48

MANLIUS

That's a nice thing to say!

CAIUS

Stow it, will you?

MARCUS

Callin' me a liar!

PUBLIUS

That'll do, that'll do. Is that why Maxentius declared war?

MARCUS (*sulkily*)

So 'e said. Playin' the dootiful son and all that. When old Galerius dies, 'e starts throwin' 'is weight about, and breakin' up Constantine's statues, and 'e teams up with Maximin Daia and starts to invade Rhaetia—only we was too quick for 'im and comes in over the Alps and catches 'im with 'is pants down at Turin.

DECIUS

Ah! More 'aste less speed. We left three-quarters of our forces on the Rhine, and there's two of them to one of us—so *they* say—and more than that, if the truth were known.

PUBLIUS

Oh, stop belly-achin'! We pasted 'em once, and we'll paste 'em again.

MANLIUS

That's right.

DECIUS

So *you* say. But mark my words——

MARCUS

Ow, come off it, can't yer?

CAIUS

Spreadin' alarm an' despondency!

MANLIUS

What's the matter with you? Got the wind up?

PUBLIUS

'Old yer bleedin' tongue, yer dirty little defeatist rat!

[*Enter* CENTURION.

49

CENTURION

Now then, what's all this noise? Corporal!

PUBLIUS

Yes, centurion. Fatigue party, centurion. Painting shields. Emperor's orders, centurion.

CENTURION

Couldn't you find a better pitch than just outside the Emperor's tent? . . . H'm. . . . (*He inspects the work.*) If you didn't talk so much you'd make a quicker job of it. Get cracking, can't you, and hold your perishing tongues.

PUBLIUS

Yes, centurion. Sorry, centurion.

CENTURION (*stabbing with his cane at one of the shields*)

That there don't look right to me. You got the perishing loop on the wrong side. Don't you know your right hand from your left? You ain't none of you got no more education than a pack of perishing monkeys.

CAIUS (*meekly*)

Didn't know it mattered which way it went. . . . What *is* it, centurion?

[*Enter* MASTER-ARMOURER, *carrying a helmet.*

CENTURION

What the 'ell's it matter to you what it is? Copy it, that's your job —and put a sock in it. . . . 'Morning, armourer.

ARMOURER

'Morning, centurion. Little rush job for the Emperor. Is His Nibs about? (*He catches sight of the shields.*) Hullo! you got it too? What's it all about, centurion?

CENTURION

Search me. . . . It ain't a regimental badge. Everybody's got to have it.

ARMOURER

Some sort of lucky charm, I expect. Sentinel said in the mess, the Emperor'd had a dream.

[*The* SOLDIERS *are all ears.*

Priests and augurs in and out of

the tent all night. (*He looks round and sees* CONSTANTINE *emerging from the tent.*) Oy, there—'shun!

[*The* SOLDIERS *scramble hurriedly to their feet and stand at attention, as* CONSTANTINE *enters, with* TOGI, GENERAL SILVIUS, *and* HOSIUS. *He is fully armed except for his helmet.*

CONSTANTINE

All right, all right, centurion. What's this? Painting-party, eh? Splendid. Let's have a look.

[*The* SOLDIERS *pick up the shields and turn them to* CONSTANTINE—*and the audience—and for the first time we see the Chi-Ro shining on them in fresh gold paint.*

Fine; fine. That'll give Maxentius something to think about.

[HOSIUS *and* TOGI *exchange a glance full of mystery and delight. The* CENTURION *and the other pagans remain stolid and uncomprehending.* By the way—ah! (*Catching sight of the* ARMOURER.) You've got it there.

[*The* ARMOURER *hands* CONSTANTINE *the helmet, which carries the Chi-Ro in brass in the place of the crest.*

Thanks. Sorry to rush you so, but you've made a very nice job of it. (*He puts it on.*)

ARMOURER

Thank you, sir.

CONSTANTINE (*to the Soldiers*)

Expect you're wondering what it all means. Well, I can tell you this much. It means there's a very great god taking a special interest in us, and we're going to give Maxentius the biggest licking he ever had in his life.

MARCUS

Hurray, sir! That's the stuff to give 'em.

[*The* SOLDIERS *applaud and the* CENTURION *glares at them.*

CONSTANTINE

Well, General, that's all clear then. You go by the Via Cassia straight to Rome. I strike off cross-country at Baccana and take the Flaminian Way. Then—we close the pincers.

GENERAL

You've got him, I think, Augustus. How much start shall you want?

51

I will address the army in an hour's time and get moving by ten sharp. You will follow at noon. Oh, and Togi! those papers . . . There's a special prayer before going into action. See that each captain has a copy and reads it to his company when the time comes.

GENERAL

Very good, Augustus.

[TOGI *hands the papers to the* GENERAL, *and also gives a copy to* HOSIUS, *who studies it carefully.*

CONSTANTINE

Now, centurion, just move the art-class a little further off, would you?

[CENTURION *removes* SOLDIERS *and their paraphernalia.*

We'll meet in Rome, General.

GENERAL

In Rome, Augustus. (*He goes out.*)

CONSTANTINE

I hope that will do, Bishop Hosius. My secretary worked it out for me—he's of your persuasion. We couldn't make it more precise. It'd upset the men to hand them out a totally unexpected and rather unconstitutional god, just before going into action. . . . Do you think it will be acceptable?

HOSIUS

Christ our God will look into the heart, my Lord Constantine, and accept what the heart has to offer Him.

CONSTANTINE

Yes. Well, I am sincerely obliged to Him, and if He gives us the victory according to promise—I liked the way He spoke, Hosius, if the vision I saw was really Him. He was very straight about it —not like the oracles, which are always right because they might mean anything. For instance, they say, "Tomorrow you will destroy a great empire", and you think it's the other man's; but if you lose, then of course it's your own and they say, "We told you so". But this wasn't at all like that. He said quite plainly: "With this sign thou shalt be victor". He couldn't go back on that, could He?

What Christ speaks, He will fulfil, for "He is faithful that promised".

CONSTANTINE

Then please assure Him, Hosius, that He will not find Constantine ungrateful. Remind Him that I have given full toleration to His followers and tell Him I intend to free His priests from a lot of taxes, and endow His churches and generally carry out His wishes, to the best of my ability. You will explain that I can't do it all at once, but if He will give me time He shall see great improvements.

HOSIUS

I will lay it all before Him in my prayers, and ask His blessing upon your arms.

CONSTANTINE

It's up to Him, then. I am sure He is a very powerful and benevolent deity, and I put my trust in Him implicitly. . . . Well, now I must get cracking. (*He moves away, turning to add*) You'll be discreet, won't you?

[*Exit* CONSTANTINE.

TOGI

O father, father! Is the great miracle really going to happen?

HOSIUS

God moves in a mysterious way, and entrusts His riches to earthen vessels. The Emperor is as ignorant as a child——

TOGI

But a little child shall lead them.

HOSIUS

"Till the kingdoms of this world shall become the Kingdom of God and of His Christ".

"And He shall reign for ever and ever".

Amen.

SCENE 5

27th October, 312—On the road to Rome (before front tabs).

[*Enter* CENTURION *and* SOLDIERS *carrying packs.*

CENTURION

Company, halt. Lay down them packs. . . . Stand at ease! . . . Now then, you! Captain's coming along to read prayers. When I says " Caps OFF " you takes 'em off on the word " off ", and stands to attention. When I says, " Company, PRAY ", on the word " pray " you elevates the 'ands and the eyes and assumes a serious and devout demeanour. . . . Oy! you there! what's that you're chewing?

1ST SOLDIER (*mumbling*)

'Andful o' corn, centurion.

CENTURION

Then spit it out or swaller it pronto, you disgusting little slobbering son of a she-camel.

[*Enter* CAPTAIN.

Company, 'shun!

CAPTAIN

All ready, centurion?

CENTURION (*with a baleful eye on* 1ST SOLDIER, *who is choking*)

Yessir.

CAPTAIN

All right, men, you can stand at ease.

[*They relax.*

Now, I don't know if you all heard what Augustus said. We're going to wait for Maxentius at a place called the Red Rocks on the Flaminian Way, about a mile this side of the Milvain Bridge. If he

takes that road out of Rome, we'll give him what he's look-
ing for. If he takes the Cassian Way, he'll run into General
Silvius and his lads. So either way we've got him, but we'll hope
he comes our way. (*Applause.*) I expect he's shaking in his shoes
and working his magicians overtime (*uneasy laughter*); but
Augustus has had a personal promise of help from the One
Great God, and has written us a special prayer to bring us luck.
So . . .

[2ND SOLDIER *clears his throat emphatically.*

Yes, my man? Did you want to ask anything?

2ND SOLDIER

Excuse me, sir. Which god would that be?

CAPTAIN (*taken slightly aback*)

Well . . . I should think perhaps it might be Olympian Jove.

[*Here* 1ST SOLDIER *becomes black in the face and is thumped on the
back by the man next him, to the* CENTURION's *great disgust.*

3RD SOLDIER

Could it be Mithras, sir? I've heard him called "The One".

4TH SOLDIER

Or the Unconquered Sun? Emperor's very partial to him, sir!

5TH SOLDIER (*eagerly*)

Or the Great Mother?

CAPTAIN (*glancing at paper in his hand*)

It doesn't say anything about a female deity.

[5TH SOLDIER *looks disappointed.*

But I should think,
if we all fixed our minds on the god or goddess of our particular
devotion, that would be the best way. . . . Very well, then.

CENTURION

Caps OFF! . . . Company, 'SHUN! . . . Company, PRAY!

[*Attitude of devotion is duly assumed.*

CAPTAIN (*reading from paper*)

God most high, to Thee we pray. Holy God, to Thee we pray.
To Thee we commend all justice; to Thee we commend our

safety; to Thee we commend our empire. In Thee we live; in Thee our victory and happiness have their being. Most high and holy God, receive our prayer. To Thee we lift our hands; hear us, we beseech Thee, O holy and most high God. (*He puts away the paper, and the* CENTURION, *who has been praying with one eye on authority, lowers his hands.*)

CENTURION

Company, 'shun!

CAPTAIN

Well, good luck to it, boys. Carry on, centurion.

CENTURION

Caps ON!... Shoulder your PACKS!... by the right, MARCH!

[*Exeunt omnes, marching. Lower lights and continue sound of tramping to suggest passage of considerable body of troops.*

Presently trumpets, followed by confused battle-noises, and shouting, which at length resolves itself into cries of "Constantine!" "Constantine!" Bring up lights and curtain together.

SCENE 6

28th October, 312—*The Imperial Palace at Rome.* (*Full set.*)

[*The scene represents one of the alae of the atrium, divided by a row of pillars on a plinth from the open court at the back, which is bathed in alternations of light and shade as clouds pass over the sun. In the court is the impluvium, with a statue, and the back-cloth shows in perspective the corresponding ala of the atrium. A few shrubs in garden-pots help to give an out-door atmosphere. The ala itself contains a table with offerings of fruit, etc. to the Lares, some trophies of arms and family busts, and an exceptionally hideous (practicable) portrait-statue of Maximian with the attributes of Hercules.*

LIVIA, *wife to Maxentius, is seated in a chair, attended by her two small* DAUGHTERS, *her* LADIES, *and female* SLAVES. *A few elderly palace* OFFICIALS *or* KNIGHTS *are sitting or standing in despondent attitudes on the plinth;* CRASSUS, *a Senator, is walking nervously up and down in the atrium;* AEMILIUS, *an aged member of the College of Augurs, leans on a staff near the table.*

Shouts of "Constantine! Constantine! Io, Constantine!" are heard dimly, off.

56

LIVIA (*a tall, dark, handsome woman, with an air of marmoreal
self-control which may hide heaven knows what*)
What are they shouting in the street? Is Constantine at the gates?

MAJOR DOMO

The gods forbid, my lady.

LIVIA

The gods will do as seems good to them. Crassus, please go and
see.

[CRASSUS *walks along towards the outer door of the atrium.*

AEMILIUS

It is very strange that we have heard no news.

KNIGHT (*with spurious cheerfulness*)

No news is good news.

LIVIA

Do you think so? A deserted palace spells the fall of princes. Ill
fortune is like the plague—wise men shun the contagion. . . . Well,
Crassus?

CRASSUS (*returning*)

I have sent for the Prefect. He is just coming in. (*He comes forward
into the ala.*)

MAJOR DOMO

Now we shall hear what's happened.

[*The* PREFECT *of the City,* ANNIUS ANULLINUS, *enters in a hurry,
looking hot and bothered.*

LIVIA

Yes, Annius Anullinus?

ANNIUS

It is nothing, madam. Some foolish citizens shouting for the
usurper. They have got it into their thick heads that he is in-
vincible.

LIVIA

So they informed the Augustus, my husband, two days ago at the
chariot-races. You should keep better order.

ANNIUS

Yes, madam. We are doing our best. (*He tries to back away, but is
detained by* CRASSUS.)

57

CRASSUS

Is it true there is fighting at the Milvian Bridge?

ANNIUS

It was reported so. About an hour ago.
  [*Uproar without.*

Forgive me, madam . . .

my duty . . . (*He hastens off.*)

KNIGHT

The Milvian Bridge is an excellent place for defence.

MAJOR DOMO

Too near the city for my liking.

KNIGHT

A single company could hold it all day.

CRASSUS

Don't be a fool, man. Maxentius went out to *attack* the enemy.
He crossed the bridge at daybreak. If he's fighting there now,
it's because he's been beaten to it.

KNIGHT

A strategic retreat, no doubt.

MAJOR DOMO

Let's hope so, let's hope so.
  [CRASSUS *walks away contemptuously.*

KNIGHT

We mustn't cross our bridges before we come to them. (*This
cliché strikes him as unfortunate, and he amends it with a nervous giggle.*)
I mean, we mustn't let Constantine cross them. . . . Take courage,
madam. . . .

LIVIA

Do I seem to you to lack courage?

AEMILIUS

The wife of Augustus sets an example to us all. But I have *every*
confidence. The omens were *most* favourable. And a prophecy was
found in the Sibylline Books that (*triumphantly*) on the 28th day of
October the enemy of Rome would be destroyed.

58

LIVIA (*with sudden vehemence*)

I hope so. I pray so. If that comes true I will offer fifty white oxen and proclaim the justice of the gods. . . . Listen!

[*A wailing outcry from the direction of the doors. An* OFFICER, *in broken and bloodstained armour, is seen staggering across the atrium, escorted by a small terrified mob of slaves, etc.*)

CRASSUS (*to the* KNIGHT)

Here comes your good news, I fancy.

[*The* OFFICER *stumbles in and kneels before* LIVIA.

LIVIA (*to the* ATTENDANTS)

Be quiet and let him speak. (*To* OFFICER) Well, sir, how has the battle gone? Is Maxentius beaten?

OFFICER

Constantine has entered the city.

LIVIA

And Maxentius?

OFFICER

Dead, madam.

LIVIA

Are you sure?

[OFFICER *sketches a gesture of assent and collapses.*

The gods have spoken. (*She veils her face. The* WOMEN *break into lamentations.*)

WOMEN (*clasping the feet of the statue*)

O Father Maximian! O god Hercules, don't desert us!

OTHERS (*at the shrine of the Lares*)

Gods of the household, defend and protect us!

DAUGHTER

O Mother, Mother! Are we all going to be killed?

[*The* LADIES *catch up the* CHILDREN *and soothe them.* CRASSUS *pours out wine for the* OFFICER, *who has been dragged into a more comfortable position down-stage, and is having his wounds dressed by a* SLAVE-GIRL.

Drink this, man.

[*Terrific noise outside and shouting for Constantine*

              Ah! the enlightened populace salutes the rising sun.

AEMILIUS

Oh, dear! oh, dear! He's here already! The gods preserve us! . . . He will have to offer sacrifices, of course. I must go and take the omens. . . . (*He hobbles out, almost cannoning into a* MESSENGER *rushing in.*)

CRASSUS

The whining, doddering, time-serving hound! He's off to propitiate fortune. (*Mimicking him*) "The omens are *most* favourable!" (*To* MESSENGER, *who has approached him*) What do *you* want?

MESSENGER (*breathless*)

My lord, you must come at once to the Capitol. Urgent summons. Meeting of the Senate. To receive the Lord Constantine.

CRASSUS

I will *not* attend the meeting. Tell them to go and bury themselves. Or if you're afraid to say that, tell them that I'm ill.

[MESSENGER *departs hurriedly.*

If they think I'm going to lick the feet of that baseborn lout of a freebooter and vote him Augustus, Princeps, First Consul and Protector of the People, they're mistaken. I'd rather cut my veins decently and ha' done with it. . . . (*To* OFFICER) Feeling better?

OFFICER

I've lost blood, that's all. Give me another drink.

CRASSUS

Here you are. . . . Now, tell us what happened.

[*All gather to listen and ejaculate, except* LIVIA, *who sits motionless.*

OFFICER

Happened? We were beaten all to blazes. . . . We left the city by the Milvian Bridge, and when we got to the fork——

MAJOR DOMO

Where the Via Cassia turns into the Via Flaminia?

OFFICER

That's it—we took the Flaminian Way. About a mile out, you come to a narrow defile between the hills and the river——

CRASSUS

I know it. The Red Rocks.

OFFICER

Constantine's men were holding it.

CRASSUS

They would be.

OFFICER

They'd got a new device on their shields—like the Greek letters Chi and Ro in a monogram (*he sketches it in the air*)—never seen such a thing before . . . it had a nasty, magical look about it.

CRASSUS

Tush, man, tush. Constantine's magic is to get there first and hit hardest. . . . Did you attack him?

OFFICER

Maxentius was in two minds . . . it's a brute of a place to force. And then, by Hades, while he was hesitating, up comes a dispatch-rider to say that the enemy had cut in behind us along the Cassian Way and had fallen on our rear above the Bridge.

CRASSUS

Oh, hell! oh, hell! oh, hell! That bloody fool Maxentius! The oldest trap in the world, and he jumps right in with both feet. He sees a road and says: "We won't go up it—so of course nobody will come down it!" Couldn't he have covered his flank? Couldn't he have—oh, Jupiter, what's the use? . . . Go on.

OFFICER

It was plain murder, that's all. Rats in a trap. No room to manœuvre. They came on in a wall of spears. We were rolled back on our own cavalry. The horses went mad. Nobody ran away

—there was nowhere to run to. One filthy jam of steel and car-
cases and bloody great thrashing hoofs. They squeezed us back
on to the bridge. Tiber was black with poor devils drowning in
their armour. I saw Maxentius flung over the parapet. He was
dead before he fell, I think . . . . Then there was a sort of great
heave and shout, and I saw Constantine on a white horse, with
the magic sign on his helmet and the banners carried before him.
The whole thing broke up, like a dam bursting. We were over the
bridge and pouring through the gates. Someone had opened
them——

CRASSUS

That blasted Prefect!

OFFICER

What the hell! The people were shouting for Constantine and, by
Mars, he deserves it. We weren't out-fought; we were out-
generalled. . . . I don't know what happened next. Everybody was
throwing away their arms. I could run at last, and I ran . . .
through the back streets up to the Palace. And here I am, and
that's all there is about it.

CRASSUS

No. As you rightly point out, there is nothing more to be said.

[*A short silence. Then the tramp of armed men approaching. As it gets
near, a burst of sunshine floods the atrium and the whole scene for the
entrance of* CONSTANTINE, *attended by* GENERAL, CAPTAIN, CENTURION,
STANDARD-BEARER *with the Labarum, and as many* SOLDIERS *as can
be mustered for the occasion. They are followed by* HOSIUS, TOGI,
AEMILIUS, ANNIUS, *and any* SENATORS *and* KNIGHTS *who may be
available. Everybody except* LIVIA *gets up and stands expectantly or
apprehensively. The* SOLDIERS, *of all ranks, form up each side to let*
CONSTANTINE *through.*

SOLDIERS

Hail, Augustus!

[CONSTANTINE *gives one glance round which takes in everything and
everybody, and comes straight down to* LIVIA.

CONSTANTINE (*very formally and politely—this is evidently
a prepared speech.*)

Madam. That my fortune should be your misfortune is the only
blot on what is, for me, a very fortunate day.

62

LIVIA (*unveiling and looking steadily at him*)
So you are Constantine.

CONSTANTINE

Yes, madam. By God's will and the fortune of war——

LIVIA (*rising*)
Is it true that you have killed my husband?

CONSTANTINE

Maxentius is dead, madam. I am grieved in your grief. (*Abandoning formality*) I really am terribly sorry.

LIVIA

Sir, I thank you. I kiss the hand of Augustus. The gods are just after all. . . . Where is Aemilius the Augur? . . . Your Sibyl spoke the truth, old man—this is the 28th of October, and the enemy of Rome is dead.
[*Everybody is stupefied.*
                    He was evil through and through—cruel to his enemies, faithless to his friends, vicious in his life, brutal in his bed. The evil was in the blood. He was a treacherous knave; Maximian his father was a treacherous old fool; Fausta, his sister, is your wife, I believe. Look to yourself.

CONSTANTINE

From another person, madam, or at another time, those words would offend us. But affliction is sacred to us, and excuses all offences.

LIVIA

Augustus is magnanimous. Sir, I have but two requests to make. The first is that I may be permitted to retire into a distant province and live privately with my daughters unmolested.

CONSTANTINE

It is granted at once, madam. I will see to it that your personal property is secured to you, together with a suitable allowance from the State funds. Pray take what attendance you please.

I am obliged to you. Secondly: I vowed that if the Sibyl spoke true I would make a thank-offering of fifty white oxen. I would like this done publicly, in Rome, by the Pontifex Maximus.

CONSTANTINE

Certainly I will do it. To what god, madam?

LIVIA

To Apollo. I thank you once more, and crave your permission to depart. (*He bows.*) Come, children.

[*She sweeps away, with her* CHILDREN *and* ATTENDANTS.

CONSTANTINE (*taking off his helmet and mopping his brow*)

Good lord deliver us! . . . Now, ladies and gentlemen, as I have been explaining to the Senate, I have won this victory by favour of the gods and in particular the God of the Christians, whose sign you see on my helmet and on these shields and things. (*Sensation.*) I understand from Bishop Hosius there that He is a God of mercy, who dislikes reprisals and so forth, so there will be a general amnesty for all those who followed Maxentius—so long, of course, as they behave themselves and don't give trouble. (*He dumps his helmet on the statue of Maximian. There is a shocked gasp, and* AEMILIUS *darts forward with a protesting croak.*) What's the matter, Aemilius? Maximian's statue? Well, I don't think the get-up suits him, and it's a shocking bad statue anyway. It probably annoyed Hercules, and that's why he didn't help you. (*His eye falls on the* OFFICER.) You all fought very well, but you weren't given a chance. Stick to me, and next time there's a dust-up I'll see you get elbow-room. (*He catches sight of* CRASSUS.) I don't think I saw you at the Senate-House just now.

CRASSUS

I have a fever, Constantine.

CONSTANTINE (*smiling*)

Let us hope it will be better tomorrow, or we shall have to see what country air will do for you.

[*This is a threat of exile.* CRASSUS, *daunted by the eye and the smile, bows sulkily.*

Now (*taking off his cloak and throw-*

ing it over the shoulders of the statue), I have a good deal of business to get through, so I needn't keep any of you people.

[*They begin to drift out.*

General! have you found the body of Maxentius?

GENERAL

Yes, Augustus. And your orders have been carried out. (*He signals to a* SOLDIER *who comes forward with* MAXENTIUS' *head on a spear.*)

[*Several more people depart in a hurry.*

CONSTANTINE

Good. Get a good big label, "Behold the head of a tyrant", and have it shown about the city. Tell the army there will be a distribution of ten gold pieces to every man—and for God's sake don't let 'em get more drunk than you can help. . . . Prefect! have you got any wild beasts in the Circus?

[*Exit* GENERAL.

ANNIUS

A fair supply, Constantine.

CONSTANTINE

Proclaim tomorrow a holiday, and put up the best show you can. . . .

[HOSIUS *whispers to him.*

What's that, Hosius? Yes, of course. . . . Nothing savage, Prefect—just beast-fights and races and some straightforward gladiator work to keep the people amused. Right you are—off with you!

[ANNIUS *goes. The room is now clear, except for* TOGI, HOSIUS, *and a couple of* SLAVES, *who are kneeling before* HOSIUS.

Who are these, Bishop? Some of your people? Run away now, little slaves, and tell your friends there's a good time coming for Christians

[*They clasp his knees gratefully.*

. . . in the West, anyhow—I can't do anything in the East—yet.

[*The* SLAVES *scuttle away.*

Come along, Hosius, we'll draft some nice

Cc   65

letters to Bishops, all about tax-exemptions and endowments. And something pretty stiff to Licinius on the subject of religious toleration. . . . Here, Togi, is there a table in this blasted barracks?

[TOGI *looks at* CONSTANTINE, *as if wondering how far he dare go with him. Then——*

TOGI

Here you are, Augustus! (*He sweeps the offerings from the table dedicated to the Lares.*)

CONSTANTINE (*leaping to catch them*)

Here, damn it! what are you doing? That's sacrilege, you little swine! You've offended all the household gods. What the devil's come over you? By Jupiter I'll—— (*He checks the blow in mid-air, and looks from the table to the Chi-Ro and back again, while a ludicrous succession of emotions—rage, alarm, shame, irritation, superstitious awe, schoolboy mischief and defiance chase one another across his face. Then he grins, and the tension is relaxed.*) Toleration, I said—not religious intolerance. Is that what happens when we stop persecuting you? Must you persecute others and break down their altars? Does your Christ want all the sky to Himself, and all the offerings too? (*He laughs a little uneasily, and looks sideways at* HOSIUS. *His tone changes.*) By the gods, I believe that's what you do want.

HOSIUS (*steadily*)

There is only one true God, my son, and He cannot be served with half-measures.

CONSTANTINE

So! . . . Well, that's logical enough, but I hadn't thought of it that way. . . . That's His strength, of course, He knows the secret of rule. One God . . . one Emperor. (*It is the birth of a new idea; he ponders it.*) One. (*He goes and stares at the Chi-Ro.*) You won our battle for us. . . . One, true, and mighty. . . . Give us Your favour and protection—and ten more years of life—— (*He turns away, discovers that he is clutching an apple in his hand, gazes at it in astonishment and takes a large bite out of it.*) All right, Togi. But do remember that, Christ or no Christ, I'm still Pontifex Maximus.

[TOGI *sets a chair at the table for him.*

Let's get on with it. Take down these letters. We'd better begin with Licinius.

ACT II

THE EMPIRE OF THE EAST

SCENE 1

March 1st, 317—The peristyle of a palace in the Balkans. (Full set.)

[*An Imperial reception is going on, and the garden is full of* FEMALE GUESTS, *among them* ZENOBIA, BERENICE, THEODOSIA, PAULINA, RHODA, CHLOE, DRUSILLA. *Various* COURT LADIES, *including* FULVIA, *are acting as hostesses, and* SLAVES *are carrying round refreshments. Down L. there is an archway, forming part of the arcade of the peristyle, which can be screened from the garden by curtains.*

ZENOBIA

Augusta always gives such charming parties. I wish I could persuade the palace cook to give me his recipe for stewed cuttle-fish.

BERENICE

I wonder if our husbands have been having the same menu. . . . Ah! Rhoda! (*To* ZENOBIA) Do you know the Prefect's wife? . . . (*To* RHODA) The Lady Zenobia. . . . I did not see you at dinner.

RHODA

Oh, no, dear Lady Berenice; we were only asked to the reception. . . . May I present my Aunt Paulina? . . . What a wonderful day it is! The Emperor Licinius and the Empress Constantia come to visit *our* Emperor and Empress—all so friendly, and the whole Empire at peace from East to West. That war was so shocking! Though I'm sure it wasn't the fault of our good Lord Constantine—he is so truly pious and Christian, though I believe not yet baptised, but I'm sure he soon will be. And it's all due to him that Licinius has stopped those dreadful persecutions in the East. Such a pity he isn't a Christian himself, poor man! We must pray for his conversion. But he doesn't bear Constantine any grudge for having beaten him, so he must be really good. And now the three darling little boys being made Caesars—such a pretty thought. . . . Do you think we shall see them?

BERENICE

You didn't go to hear them proclaimed?

RHODA

Oh, I left that to my husband—so public, and such a crowd!

FULVIA

The Imperial Party will be coming out presently. . . . You have nothing to eat or drink. . . . Slaves! Cakes and wine for the Prefect's lady.

CHLOE (*to* DRUSILLA)

What an extraordinary collection of people one meets at the Palace nowadays!

DRUSILLA

When emperors patronise a slave-religion, one must expect society to be made up of freedmen and shopkeepers.

CHLOE

We must accept what Fate sends us, I suppose. Licinius——

DRUSILLA

Licinius has made his throw for power and lost the game. How long will he endure against this Emperor of the Plebs, with his jealous God and his devouring ambition?

CHLOE

Are the gods dead, that they no longer come to defend their altars?

DRUSILLA

Epicurus said that the gods knew nothing of men. Philosophy is all that is left to us. . . .

[*They pass on into the garden.*

THEODOSIA

. . . so let us hope Licinius continues in his present good frame of mind.

ZENOBIA

Our new Caesars, at any rate, should not prove formidable tyrants.

THEODOSIA

True. But my husband says he wonders what the Empire is coming to when it has to get its Caesars from the nursery. Crispus, he says, is all very well. He is twelve years old, and will soon put on discretion with his manly-gown. But the little Licinius is an infant in arms.

[MATIBENA *comes, with* SLAVES, *to set chairs and purple cushions below the archway.*

ZENOBIA

He is his father's only boy. And if Constantine's son is to be made Caesar—why, so must the son of Licinius.

THEODOSIA

Yes, I see that. But why make a Caesar of the baby Constantine?

ZENOBIA

To please Augusta. *Crispus* is the child of Constantine's *first* wife. And if *her* son is to be Caesar, Fausta's must be Caesar too.

BERENICE

Augusta is jealous?

ZENOBIA

Let us say that Augustus is just. . . . My husband rather agrees with yours, Theodosia. But he says one can scarcely blame Constantine for choosing Caesars who can't give trouble. Look at that man Bassianus! Just to please Licinius, Constantine gives him his sister Anastasia in marriage, and makes him Caesar of Italy—and what happens? He intrigues with his brother, who's one of Licinius's people, starts a rebellion, gets himself executed— Licinius takes the matter up, and starts a war—in which, thank goodness, he got the worst of it. As if we hadn't had wars enough, and rival Emperors enough, in the bad old days.

BERENICE

Well! Nobody can say Constantine hasn't done all he can to please Licinius.

PAULINA

He's done far too much. How long will he halt between two opinions? If he were sincere in his Christian professions, he would break down these heathen temples, uproot the altars, and banish the worship of devils through the length and breadth of the West.

RHODA

Oh, Auntie! I don't think that would do!

69

FULVIA

Please be careful. Many of our guests are of the old religion.

RHODA

Isn't it enough that we can at last worship in peace and safety?
Let us be thankful for God's mercies and ask no more.

PAULINA (*ignoring* RHODA)

And there's another thing—why does he let that heathen woman
dance attendance upon the Augusta? (*To* FULVIA) You belong
to the Court—you know who I mean.

FULVIA (*uncomfortably*)

Bassiana Marcia?

PAULINA

Yes. She's the sister of the rebel Caesar, and she's a rebel herself
and a spy, as well as a rank heathen. Her husband, who is a very
decent man—my late husband did a lot of business in Rome and
knew him well—he divorced her when he found out what she
was up to, and she ought to have been sent into exile.

FULVIA

She is a very close friend of Augusta.

PAULINA

That is what I am complaining of. . . . Oh, you ladies take things
so easily. You follow the fashion and sun yourselves in the
Emperor's favour.

[MATIBENA, *who has missed nothing of this conversation, hobbles away
in the direction of the Palace.*

But the evil days may return. There are
martyrs in my family. This bone (*she touches a reliquary at her neck*)
bore witness to Christ in the arena under Diocletian.

BERENICE

Dear madam, you make us all feel very humble. But we must
hope that the Empress will convert her friend.

RHODA

Don't let us spoil this lovely day with anxieties! . . . Look! there's
a bustle—I think they'll be coming out soon.

Yes, they won't be long now.

[*The party in the garden is beginning to line itself up expectantly.*

RHODA

Let's get a good place in the front. I do so want to see the darling babies.

DRUSILLA

Come, Chloe, we must salute the sucking tyrants. Caligula the Tyrant made a senator of his horse, and Constantine the Christian makes Caesars in swaddling-clothes. Autocrats tolerate no power but their own.

[*Flourish. Enter from the Palace the* AUGUSTI CONSTANTINE *and* LICINIUS: *the* AUGUSTAE FAUSTA *and* CONSTANTIA; HELENA; *the* 12-year-old CAESAR CRISPUS *with his tutor* LACTANTIUS; *the two infant* CAESARS CONSTANTINE *and* LICINIUS *with their* NURSES; MARCIA; HOSIUS; *and other* LORDS, LADIES *and* ATTENDANTS.

GUESTS

Hail Augustus! Hail Caesar! . . . Oh, the darlings! aren't they sweet! . . . How beautiful our Empress is! There's the Empress Constantia! Isn't she like her brother? Look at Crispus in his purple cloak—his father all over again . . . (*and a good deal more of the same sort of thing*).

CHLOE

O gods! Is somebody going to make a speech?

DRUSILLA

It's that dreadful old man Lactantius—a rabid Christian; he wrote a horrid book, called "The Deaths of the Persecutors"—all slanders against the Emperors from beginning to end. He's been made tutor to young Crispus.

CHLOE

How disgusting!

LACTANTIUS (*taking the floor and bowing to the Imperial Family*)

Our two Augusti, reigning hand-in-glove,
With their two ladies bound in mutual love,

71

Now to the purple add three Caesars more,
Like Graces three combined with Virtues four;
Even so the rainbow with its sevenfold band
Extends its promised peace from east to western land.

[*Applause.*

CONSTANTINE

Well rhymed, old philosopher. I didn't know you were a poet as
well as a divine and a historian and all the rest of it.

LICINIUS

Very neat, by Apollo! Worthy of Horace himself.

CRISPUS

That was a splendid compliment, Lactantius. Nice and short.
We will excuse you from giving us our lessons tomorrow.

[*Everybody laughs.* LACTANTIUS *is smiled on by the* EMPRESSES
and bows himself away to HELENA's *side.*

HELENA

Very tactfully phrased, Lactantius.

LACTANTIUS

I trust it was acceptable. There are Scriptural allusions in it for
such as have ears.

[*The Imperial Party has now arrived at the archway.*

FAUSTA

Come and sit down for a little before the entertainment begins.
These parties are so tiring.

CONSTANTIA

What are you giving us, Constantine?

CONSTANTINE

Music; a little tumbling and dancing; and a recitation from Virgil.

LICINIUS

I'm glad your religious toleration extends to the Muses.

CRISPUS

Lactantius says Virgil was a prophet of Christ. We're having the
Fourth Eclogue. (*He declaims.*)

Lo! foretold by the Sibyl, the fulness of time is upon us,
Fresh from the start, new-born, is the mighty order of ages;
Now shall the Virgin return and the great Saturnian kingdom,
Now from the height of the heavens descends the renewer, the
                                                    First-Born.

[FAUSTA *looks at* CRISPUS *with irritation.*

LICINIUS

Bravo, young man! I see we shall have no need of a rhapsodist.

CRISPUS

I know lots of Virgil.

CONSTANTINE

Another time, my boy. Go along now with Lactantius.

CONSTANTIA

We will come and hear you tomorrow.

[*The three* CAESARS *depart with* LACTANTIUS *and the* NURSES.

FAUSTA (*taking* MARCIA *by the arm, and detaching her from the other* LADIES)

Come Marcia. Give me some wine. I am quite exhausted.

HELENA

Oh, Fausta dear, let us dismiss our attendants and wait on ourselves. It is so pleasant to be just the family party. (*To* MARCIA)
Please draw the curtain as you go.

[*Exit* MARCIA.

FAUSTA

Why do I have to be publicly snubbed like that?

HELENA

My dear, it is not very wise to be conspicuously intimate with
one person rather than another. It causes comment.

FAUSTA

How do you know? I suppose that tiresome old servant of yours
has been listening and prying as usual. . . . If you want me to get

rid of poor Marcia, Constantine, why don't you say so, instead of leaving it all to your mother?

CONSTANTINE

My dear, I have never demanded any such thing. But as regards showing favouritism, I think my mother is right.

FAUSTA

Oh, she's always right, of course. But who started making favourites? I didn't ask you to promote Bassianus and marry him to your sister Anastasia. You did that to please yourself or to please Licinius.

LICINIUS

Please don't bring me into it.

FAUSTA

You told me then to give Marcia a place at court and make a friend of her. So I did—just to please *you*. If you made a stupid mistake about Bassianus, that wasn't my fault—or Marcia's either. And anyhow, I thought the whole idea was to be friends all round and let bygones be bygones. If Marcia can overlook the fact that you had her brother executed, I should have thought you could manage to do the same—even if it was only part of the business of making it up with Licinius.

LICINIUS (*laughing*)

I assure you, the re-instatement of Bassiana Marcia formed no part of the peace-treaty conditions.

FAUSTA

It wouldn't. You don't care what happens to people. When Constantine wanted to please *you*, I was ordered to be friends with Marcia. Now that *you* want to please Constantine, I'm ordered to give her up. Nobody considers *my* feelings.

CONSTANTINE

You're getting worked up about nothing, my dear. You haven't been asked to dismiss Marcia—only to be a little less demonstrative in public.

[*Flutes play. The* GUESTS *begin to move off towards the Palace.*

Licinius, would you like to come and see the players

74

before the show begins? There is a pair of acrobats of great talent. You might think it worth while to invite them to Byzantium. . . .

[CONSTANTINE *and* LICINIUS *thankfully make their escape.*

FAUSTA

There! he's always like that. Nothing I say is of any importance. I do everything I can to please him, and he just takes it for granted. When poor Papa tried to assassinate him, I was a good wife, wasn't I? I told him all about it—and sometimes I wish I hadn't —and he had Papa strangled and seemed to think I ought to be pleased about it. And then he killed my brother Maxentius, and had his head carried all round Rome stuck on a horrid pole, and when I cried he said it was all the fortune of war. And he insisted on my being a Christian, which I'm sure I never wanted to be. And now (*to* HELENA) you want me to get rid of my only real friend, and he backs you up——

HELENA

Dear Fausta, I'm very sorry I spoke. I didn't mean that at all.

FAUSTA

I don't care what you meant. It's Constantine. . . . Yes, yes, I know—he gives me children and he's faithful to me, and I don't have to put up with scandal and orgies and concubines. But it's only because he thinks God likes him to be respectable. He hasn't got any feelings—it's all policy, policy, policy.

CONSTANTIA

Oh, Fausta! The lives of princes are not their own—they belong to the Empire. God's Empire first, and, for the sake of that, to the Empire of the world. I am a Christian, wedded to a heathen husband—not by my choice, yet willingly, if that may bring the Empire to Christ. Or if not, willingly all the same, since it might have been so, and it was right to try. So it is with my sister Anastasia: the hope of peace wedded her to Bassianus, and the necessity of peace unwedded her; and she endures judgment as she may, trusting that I or another may do what she might not. Our Lady Helena too endured to be parted from my father, whom she dearly loved, in order that his son and hers might come to be Christ's first Emperor in Rome. Neither can Constantine live for himself, but to the duty to which he is called. The hard way is often the necessary way; and the hardest of all is the way that seems to lead nowhere, and the suffering that seems to fulfil no need. To be torn between father and husband, between husband and brother, and not to know the end or dare to choose. To see the danger and have no right to warn—to keep silence and to wait.

FAUSTA (*petulantly, but a little subdued all the same*)

You are just like Constantine. You haven't any heart—it's all duty and destiny. And you wait here, with your terrible calculating patience, like a cat in a corner, for God to send you a mouse. . . . Do you think He has a mouse for me? . . . Mamma, I am sorry I made a scene. Constantine hates scenes—please tell him not to be angry.

[*Enter* MARCIA, *with some* SLAVES *attending her.*

MARCIA (*drawing back the curtain*)

Madam, the entertainers await Your Imperial Majesties' pleasure.

FAUSTA

We are quite ready. (*She makes to take* MARCIA's *arm, recollects herself, and goes out by herself through the archway,* MARCIA *standing aside for her.*)

HELENA (*pausing to gather up a wrap*)

What danger do you foresee, Constantia?

CONSTANTIA

I cannot say. But I wish you had spoken to her alone.

HELENA

Did I humiliate her too much, poor child?

CONSTANTIA

That was not what I had in mind.

HELENA

I see. . . .

[*They look at one another with perfect understanding.*

May God be with you, Constantia. . . . Yes, Fausta, we are coming.

[*They go out; and the* SLAVES *who came with* MARCIA *remove the chairs, etc., from the forestage.*

76

March 2nd, 317—A place in the palace. (Before tabs.)

[*Enter* LICINIUS *and* MARCIA.

LICINIUS

You understand what has to be done.

MARCIA

Perfectly, Augustus.

LICINIUS

Play on her jealousy—of her stepson Crispus——

MARCIA

That is easy, for she hates him.

LICINIUS

And of her husband's work and interests——

MARCIA

That is easier still, for she is in love with him.

LICINIUS

And of the new religion.

MARCIA

That is more difficult, because she cares little either way. Her religion is the worship of Augusta.

LICINIUS

Tell her to make offerings to Aphrodite. Be discreet. Take your time. I must wait before I can strike, because we must not risk another failure. But your brother shall be avenged and the old worship restored—I promise you that, Bassiana Marcia.

MARCIA

Count on me.

[*Exeunt.*

77

SCENE 3

A.D. 323—*A house in Rome.* ($\frac{1}{2}$ *set A.*)

[A number of persons have been invited to a poetry-reading, among them CRASSUS *and* BASSIANA MARCIA. *The room is dimly lit by two small lamps for the reader's use. Night-sky seen through window.*

HOST

Ladies and gentlemen. In this the 13th year of Constantine and Licinius Augusti, the thousand and eighty-fifth from the founding of the City, or—as it is becoming fashionable to say—the three hundred and twenty-third of the Christian era (*a contemptuous laugh*) it is agreeable to remind ourselves that the cult of the Muses is not altogether abandoned in Rome. This evening, one of the most elegant of our younger poets—you have met him at dinner, so I need not introduce him (*applause and laughter*)—will gratify our little circle with a reading of his eclogue. (*Applause.*) He tells me that though classical in style it is modern and topical in content. It takes the form of an amoeboean contest; it starts without preliminary, and you yourselves are to adjudge the prize to the successful shepherd. The part of Mopsus will be read by our old friend Laelius Gallus (*applause*) and that of Thyrsis by the poet himself (*loud applause*) . . . I hope those lights are right for you both. . . . Mopsus is the challenger and begins.

LAELIUS (*reading*)

Age is better than youth; let lads go sweat at the plough-tail,
Or craze their wits for Chloe; snug in the night I pile up
Resinous logs, hob-nob with the little gods of the fireside,
Loosed from labour, safe from the mischievous son of the Cyprian.

POET (*reading*)

Autumn is better than spring; spring is the season of fevers,
Disasters at lambing-time, treacherous winds from the mountains,
Hunger of heart: bring wine, October! blot from remembrance
Dank earth, the moss-grown altar, the clammy odour of toad-
stools.

LAELIUS (*reading*)

New times for old: new men, new taxes, new regulations,
New city-fashions; but still my pipe makes shift with the old tunes;

Mincius runs through the reeds as of yore; the bull seeks the heifer,
Grain yellows, our goats give milk, the olives ooze from the oil-
press.

POET (*reading*)

New gods for old; for the lyre of Apollo the howling of hymn-tunes
Makes exchange; for the saffron veil, sackcloth, and ashes for
garlands,
For the cry of the amorous nymph in the brake and the satyr
pursuing,
The voices of angry old men arguing in Alexandria.

[½ *set B is lit up—a room in Alexandria.*

ALEXANDER

No, no, Arius, it will not do. Every bishop in Egypt has pro-
nounced against you.

ARIUS

I do not care. You may excommunicate me if you choose. There
are other bishops. Eusebius of Nicomedia is on my side, and
Eusebius of Caesarea. I have letters from Lydda, Tyre, Berytus,
Laodicea and Anazarbus—I can count on the support of the
whole Eastern Church. I shall appeal to them—and I shall tell
them that the doctrine that I taught was learnt from you.

ALEXANDER

Never—nothing that I have ever said could be interpreted to
mean that Our Lord the Word is not perfect God.

ARIUS

I agree that He is perfect God, unchangeable, and that He was
not made out of any pre-existing subject, but by the will and
design of the Father He began to be before all time and before all
ages. But since you will hardly say that He is unbegotten——

ALEXANDER

He is begotten of the Father——

ARIUS

Therefore the Father is before Him. And I say that before the Son
was generated or created——

79

He was *not* created.

ARIUS (*shouting them down*)

. . . before He was derived, or decreed or founded or whatever word you like, He was not, since He is not unbegotten.

ATHANASIUS

Have you no ideas in your head except an earthly begetting and the birth of man's flesh? God knows no times nor seasons, and the begetting of the Son is of eternity.

ARIUS

You make free with your tongue, little Deacon Athanasius, in the presence of your spiritual superiors. But I tell you——

ALEXANDER

And I tell you, Arius, that your doctrine is heresy, and that by the authority of this synod you are excommunicated and deprived of your office, you and your followers Achillas, Carpones, Aeithales, Sarmatas, and the deacons Euzoius, Lucius, Julius, Menas. . . .

[*Fade out light and sound on $\frac{1}{2}$ set B.*

POET (*reading*)

Return, return, Eurydice, look not back; Persephone
Return to us, and return in the hyacinth-season Adonis;
Return O sky-gods, earth-gods, sea-gods; have you all eaten
The fatal pomegranate-seed in the house of Plutonian Hades?

GUESTS

Delightful. . . . Too Virgilian. . . . Oh, no, dear, not *Virgil*, he's so out of date . . . deliciously melancholy . . . so sarcastic. . . . Well, I give the prize to Mopsus—I'm all for making the best of a bad government. . . . Thyrsis has my vote. . . . I like those unorthodox rhythms . . . so true about this vulgar new religion. . . .

CRASSUS

Very nice verses, I dare say, but the trouble is, these vulgar Christians are alive and you're not. They bother about their repulsive God. They quarrel and shout and throw brickbats in His holy name. Do you shoot as much as a dried pea in the defence of the Archer-goddess? Do you clout people over the head for confusing the Persian Mithras with Phoebus Apollo? Not you. All you do is to go about in white togas, striking appropriate attitudes.

LAELIUS

Come, come, Crassus—it's no good getting worked up about it.

POET

You'd better migrate to the east. Licinius is taking order there with the Christians.

CRASSUS

Yes—and Constantine is besieging him, horse, foot and artillery in Byzantium. Are you doing anything about it? Eclogues and elegiacs—not so much as a whiff of protest, let alone an insurrection or a——

POET

Well, it's the Senate's business. You're a senator—you'd better start something there.

CRASSUS

The Senate? Bah! . . . I'm fed up. I'm going. . . . If anybody likes to lay an information against me, good luck to it.

[*He starts to go. The party is thrown into confusion.* MARCIA *catches* CRASSUS *at the door.*

MARCIA

If you want to pull down Constantine, there are more ways than one of setting about it.

CRASSUS

What's that? Bassiana Marcia? I thought you were with Augusta.

MARCIA

I am sent to Rome by Augusta. Even women can feel resentment. Come and see me. . . . There may be something for you to do.

81

A.D. 324—*A camp before the walls of Byzantium. Evening.*

[*Enter two* SENTRIES *meeting.*

1ST SENTRY

All quiet?

2ND SENTRY

Too damn quiet. I hate this cursed siege-work. Digging all night and push and go all day, and nothing to show for it.

1ST SENTRY

Byzantium's a hard place to take.

2ND SENTRY

What's the good of beleaguering a place that gets all its supplies by sea? We sit here banging at the front door while they pop in and out by the back, laughing at us. If ever we see the inside of the place you can call me Christian.

1ST SENTRY

I will—and don't you forget it. I'm putting my faith in God and the fleet.

2ND SENTRY

I'd put more faith in the fleet if we had a more experienced admiral. A lad of nineteen that's never seen salt water——

[*A cry within, R.*

Now what's up with the garrison?

1ST SENTRY (*looking off R.*)

Nothing doing that I can see. Crispus is young, but there's good stuff in him. He's a chip of the old block.

2ND SENTRY

That's not much help against odds of three to one.

1ST SENTRY

They say it ain't ships as counts so much as the way you handle them. My cousin that's seen a power o' sea-fighting says Licinius has made a bad mistake. Says he ought to have attacked in the Aegean, instead of letting his ships get bottled up in the Straits.

2ND SENTRY

Arm-chair strategy. All I know is——

1ST SENTRY

Well, it's common sense, ain't it? Same as on land. Like getting your troops squeezed in a mountain-pass, the way Maxentius did when we hammered him at the Red Rocks.

2ND SENTRY

That was before my time. Anyhow I don't hold with salt water—nasty treacherous stuff, all oops-a-daisy and tastes filthy. And you're catting all the time. If I gotter fight, I like to know where me legs and stomach have got to——

[*Enter* MESSENGER *running.*

SENTRIES

Halt! Who goes there?

MESSENGER

Friend. Take me to the Emperor. Quick. I'm from the fleet.

1ST SENTRY

What news?

MESSENGER

Crispus has forced the Hellespont.

2ND SENTRY

Well I'll be—baptised!

1ST SENTRY

Praise God!

[*More cries within.*

2ND SENTRY

There's hell to pay in the city.

1ST SENTRY

Take him with you to the Emperor's tent——

[*Exeunt* 2ND SENTRY *and* MESSENGER, *L.*

(*shouting after them*)—and then come back for the christening!
(*He takes up his sentry-beat.*) Good old Crispus! Good old Constantine! Good old Navy! Good old heavenly Providence! . . .

[*Exit, R.*

SCENE 5

A.D. 324—*A tented field before Chrysopolis. On the R. the tent of*
CONSTANTINE, *on the L. the tent of* LICINIUS. *Night.* (*Full set.*)

[*Enter R.* TOGI *armed and* CRISPUS *overtaking him.*

CRISPUS

Is that you, Togius? Where is my father?

TOGI

In the tent, Caesar, praying to the God of battles to inspire his
strategy tomorrow.

CRISPUS

I'll join him there. . . . You are looking very warlike.

TOGI

I asked Augustus to give me some fighting to do. I feel ashamed—
a great able-bodied fellow like me—with nothing in my hand
but a stilus. He has allowed me to be one of the special guard that
protects the sacred standard.

CRISPUS

That's a great honour. They are all picked men. Are you so good
a swordsman?

TOGI

I know how to fight. And then, you see, I am a Christian from
birth. Only real, proper Christians are chosen to defend the
Labarum. We have to carry it to any part of the field where
danger threatens. But the soldiers say it is not we who guard it,
but that it guards us. It turns aside all weapons. There was a
standard-bearer once who lost his nerve and let it go, and he was
shot through the body immediately.

You'll stick to it, I'm sure—as faithfully as you have stuck to my father. You've come a long way, Togius, from your little island on the edge of the world—right across the Western Empire.

TOGI

And now we have passed the Hellespont and stand in the East. Constantine will go farther yet, and I with him, please God.

CRISPUS

Yes; Licinius is beaten—and knows it. His camp seems quiet enough.

TOGI

We have sent a spy to find out their positions. But, do what they may, tomorrow we shall take Chrysopolis.

CRISPUS

Let us go and pray for victory.

[TOGI *lifts the flap of the tent, showing a lighted altar, with* CONSTANTINE, HOSIUS, *and others kneeling. He goes in with* CRISPUS, *and the flap closes.*

[*Enter, from his tent,* LICINIUS *with a* GENERAL, *an* AUGUR *and two* SOOTHSAYERS.

LICINIUS (*to* AUGUR)

You say the omens are good. You said that before; yet our fleet was destroyed in the Hellespont and Byzantium fell. (*To* SOOTHSAYERS) You have brought the gods from Egypt to aid the Lords of Olympus, yet neither magic nor prayers hold back the advance of Constantine. How have I offended? I and mine worship as our fathers did and honour the ancestral deities. Constantine is an atheist, without reverence or piety, disgracing the army with the symbol of this upstart godling whom he has raised up from the gutter and the gallows. Why does Heaven favour him rather than me? Are the gods impotent? Or are my priests polluted, my soothsayers all liars, and my generals cowardly and incompetent? (*Deprecatory murmurs.*) I tell you if we do not do better tomorrow, we have lost the last throw, and there will be nothing for it but to abandon the gods who have abandoned us, and do homage to their new-fangled conqueror—who seems at least to have the ability and the will to do something in return for his offerings.

Sir, the will of the gods is our fate, and no one can fight against it. But your army has done nothing to deserve harsh words. What man can do, we shall do tomorrow. We shall attack Constantine wherever we find him, and pierce a path through the thickest of his guard; and if we do not bring him to your Majesty alive or dead, we will go down to the gods of the dead, who shall need no other sacrifice.

LICINIUS

Send Constantine's men there before you, and glut their altars. But avoid that standard of his. It is magical. It blasts at a touch. Cut down its guards; but lay no hand on it or on the standard-bearer.

GENERAL

If you say so, Licinius. It's a pity these gentlemen can't find a spell to counter it.

1ST SOOTHSAYER

I have cursed it by the gods of the upper world and the nether: by Isis and Osiris, by Anubis and Thoth, by Horus and Set and Serapis; I have cursed it by Ammon and Bubastes, by Baal and Reseph and Astarte——

2ND SOOTHSAYER

I have cursed it by the Sun and Moon and the Seven Dancers; I have cursed it by earth, air, fire and water; by Dis and the Dirae and by the three-headed porter at the gates of Hell. I have cursed it——

GENERAL

I would rather curse it by sword and spear and javelin. But if it is an order——

LICINIUS

It is an order. Go and get some rest. I will address the army at day-break. . . . And you, return, and deafen the ears of the gods. . . . Good night.

ALL

Good night, Augustus, and good fortune.

[*Exeunt* LICINIUS *into his tent, and the others, severally, L.*

[*Enter from his tent* CONSTANTINE *with* CRISPUS, HOSIUS, TOGI, *and a* GENERAL.

CONSTANTINE (*cheerfully*)

Well, we shall add to our laurels tomorrow. That strategy will work, General . . . it came to me like an answer to prayer. It *was* an answer to prayer. . . . See that the men have double rations for breakfast and be ready to move an hour before dawn.

[*Enter a* SPY.

Well my lad, and what do you want? Oh, it's the spy we sent out. What is Licinius doing?

SPY

Mostly cursing, sir. Him and his magicians have been holding religious services solid for the last two hours, wishing you and the sacred standard to 'ell, sir, if you'll excuse the expression. They expect you to attack after sunrise, sir, and they think you'll start with a cavalry charge on their centre.

CONSTANTINE

Do they? They had better think again. Well done. Go and tell General Silvius all about it.

[*Exeunt* GENERAL *and* SPY.

Tomorrow we set up Christ's standard over the East. Togi, are all the letters and proclamations ready for dispatch?

TOGI

Yes, Augustus. And if I am killed, Lucius has full instructions.

CONSTANTINE

What is it, Crispus? Do you think I am counting my chickens before they are hatched?

CRISPUS (*a little uneasily*)

The heathen would call it unlucky.

HOSIUS

They would call it presumption. But our God is not jealous of His children, but only for His own honour.

CONSTANTINE

He has called me to be His viceroy, and He will not abandon me before my task is done. Twice He has shown me His sign. The

87

first time in Gaul, written in light and fire across the face of the sun.

HOSIUS

You never told me that, sir.

CONSTANTINE

"Air and fire in Gaul"—where have I heard that before? . . . I did not tell you, Bishop, because I did not want to prejudice you. For the second time the sign was shown me in my dreams before the Battle of the Milvian Bridge, and you interpreted it to me when all my priests and diviners were dumb. . . . I took it for a token from the One True God, whom my father Constantius honoured by the name of the Unconquered Sun. But you said the symbol stood for the name of Christ.

HOSIUS

He is called "the Day-spring" and "the Sun of Righteousness".

CONSTANTINE

So, as soon as I was master of the West, I set the Unconquered Sun upon my Imperial coins, thinking: "that will be a parable for the wise to interpret. The people will take it to be Phoebus Apollo; but Christ, if He be indeed the One God, will know that it is meant for Him". And now tomorrow, when He has made me master of the world, I vow that I will speak no more in parables. The Unconquered Sun shall vanish from the coins, and the sign of Christ shall be set there openly. And there shall be one Empire, and one Christ over all the Empire. So help me God.

HOSIUS, CRISPUS, TOGI

Amen.

CRISPUS

Father, I have made no will—all that I have is yours. But I should like to dedicate to the Church my share of the spoils of battle. And Togi, if I should fall, send my finger-ring and my brooch, with my dutiful love, to the Lady Fausta my step-mother.

CONSTANTINE

Is there no girl with a better claim to them, my boy?

CRISPUS

Not yet.

88

You astonish me. At your age I had a dozen . . . The Bishop looks shocked. It was before you took charge of my morals, Hosius. . . . Come now, Gemini is on the horizon, it is getting late. . . . A little sleep, and then—Chrysopolis!

SCENE 6

A battlefield. (Before tabs.)

[*Noise of fighting off L. Enter* SOLDIER, *running.*

SOLDIER

Ho, there! send reinforcements! The Labarum to aid! The Emperor's down—his horse killed under him. To Constantine! To Constantine!

[*He runs off, shouting, R. Enter L.* SOLDIERS *fighting confusedly.* CONSTANTINE'S *men being driven across the stage.*

CONSTANTINE'S GENERAL

Christ to our aid! Stick to it, lads. Give it 'em back! (*etc. etc.*)

ENEMY SOLDIERS

Strike! strike, by Mars! Down with him! Help Hercules! (*etc. etc.*)

[*Enter R.* SOLDIERS *with the Labarum borne by a* STANDARD-BEARER, *and* TOGI *among them. They fall on* LICINIUS' MEN, *who recoil from the Labarum and are driven out. One* ENEMY *makes a snatch at the standard and is cut down by* TOGI. *Shouting off. Re-enter* TOGI *to wounded* ENEMY, *who is struggling to his feet.*

TOGI

Come on, my battle-trophy! I need a new helmet.

[*Exit, lugging him in.*

SCENE 7

A.D. 324—*Nicomedia—A room in the palace.* (½ *set.*)

VOICE (or VOICES) (*proclaiming behind the curtain*)

Flavius Valerius Constantinus Maximus, Emperor of the East, Emperor of the West, sole Augustus, pious, happy, victorious, triumphant, Germanicus, Sarmaticus, Francicus, Gothicus, Vandalicus, Pontifex Maximus, Tribune of the People, eight times Consul. . . .

TOGI'S VOICE (*reading*)

"Victor Constantinus Maximus Augustus . . ."

[*The curtain rises.* CONSTANTINE *at a table listening to the draft* TOGI *is reading aloud.* HOSIUS *and* LACTANTIUS *in attendance.*

CONSTANTINE

Yes, yes. We know that bit.

TOGI (*reading*)

". . . to the pious and reverend fathers, Alexander Bishop of Alexandria . . ." *

CONSTANTINE

—and the irrepressible and infuriating ex-priest Arius! Get on, get on, cut out the flourishes. I shall lose my temper in a moment.

TOGI (*reading*)

"I call God to witness that my chief reason in undertaking my late victorious campaign was to heal the dissensions lately risen among you. For a spirit of controversy——"

CONSTANTINE

Not strong enough. "An intolerable frenzy."

TOGI (*amending his draft*)

"—an intolerable frenzy having seized on all Africa through the wicked frivolity of those who seek to split up the worship of the peoples into schismatical sects, I could find no cure for the plague but to expel the common enemy of the world, who was opposing his lawless will to your sacred counsels". (*He pauses and looks up inquiringly.*)

LACTANTIUS

Excuse me, Augustus. Are you making Licinius to blame for the Donatist controversy? It really started before his time, with the persecutions of Diocletian.

HOSIUS

You are a historian, Lactantius. No one could speak with more authority than the author of "The Deaths of the Persecutors".

But I apprehend Augustus to mean that the trouble arose from the presence of a heathen and persecuting emperor in the East—whether Licinius or another.

CONSTANTINE

That's exactly what I mean. By the way, Lactantius, you'll have to revise that tenth chapter of yours, celebrating Licinius as the white hope of oriental Christendom.

LACTANTIUS

I am doing so, Augustus. It is a pity he didn't go on as he began. He promised well.

CONSTANTINE

Every time I beat him he promised. Every time I forgave him he broke his promise. He was always a persecutor at heart. He won't get another opportunity—though I suppose I shall have to forgive him again. (*To* TOGI) Didn't you say there was a suppliant waiting in the antechamber?

TOGI

Yes, Augustus—a lady closely veiled.

CONSTANTINE

I will see her in a minute. Go on with the letter.

TOGI (*reading*)

"Filled with the highest hopes I came to the East, as to the very home of the Christian faith. Bitter was my disappointment to find it even more rent by divisions than the West—the more so when I discovered how extremely trifling was the matter at issue between you."

LACTANTIUS

What *is* the dispute, Hosius? Another quarrel about ecclesiastical appointments?

HOSIUS

No, I think this time it is about doctrine.

CONSTANTINE

Some fantastic quibble which nobody can make head or tail of; I'm coming to that.

TOGI (*reading*)

"This is the cause of the dispute, as I understand it. You, Alexander, asked each of your priests what he thought about some passage in the Scriptures, or rather about some minor point of interpretation. You, Arius, imprudently came out with an opinion which ought never to have entered your head—or, if it did, ought not to have been uttered. And this led to a breach between you and refusal of communion, so that the faithful were set by the ears and the harmony of the body destroyed."

CONSTANTINE

That's forcible, don't you think?

LACTANTIUS

Admirably so, Augustus. Which is the passage in question?

TOGI (*referring to a letter*)

The eighth chapter of Proverbs. About the eternal generation of the Word.

LACTANTIUS

Oh, I see. (*He exchanges glances with* HOSIUS.)

TOGI (*reading*)

"Now take my advice——" Pardon me, Augustus, is that just a trifle abrupt? Might it be more elegant to say: "Let both of you, in an equal spirit of forbearance, accept the fair-minded advice of——"

CONSTANTINE

"—of your divinely appointed Emperor". Because God *has* appointed me.

HOSIUS

Most true. But I was about to suggest, " of your fellow-servant".

CONSTANTINE

"Of your——?" Oh, I see what you mean. Like the Angel in the Revelation. "I am thy fellow-servant." Yes—of course that's also true, if you look at it that way. And it sounds very becoming. Thank you, Bishop.

TOGI (*writing it in*)

"—advice of your fellow-servant, which is that questions of this kind ought not to be asked in the first place, and not answered if they are, being quite unnecessary and calculated only to amuse idle minds. Or, if they are intended as an academic exercise, they should be argued in private, and not published abroad to disturb the faith of the simple-minded."

CONSTANTINE

I've got them there, I fancy.

TOGI (*reading*)

"Pray consider that philosophers of the same school, though they may dispute about details, are able to agree upon their fundamental beliefs; how much more should we, the servants of the great God, preserve harmony among ourselves!"

CONSTANTINE

And I hope they take it to heart. All this wrangling and fighting makes us a laughing-stock. "How these Christians love one another!"—that's what the heathen say, and I don't blame them.

HOSIUS

It is most unfortunate.

CONSTANTINE

It's wicked. It's ungrateful. It's abominable. It makes me sick. I've told 'em so. Go on, Togi.

TOGI (*reading*)

"Give me back my peaceful nights and days, that I may take pleasure in the sunlight and enjoy a tranquil life from now on. Imagine my distress—only yesterday, when I set foot in Nicomedia, my mind was set on pressing forward to the East. But just as I was starting to come to you, the news of this trouble reined back my purpose, that I might not be compelled to see with my eyes what I felt I could not endure to hear with my ears. Come to an agreement, and so open to me the road of the East which your quarrels have closed against me."

A most moving peroration, Augustus.

CONSTANTINE

It really is heart-breaking—after all I've done for them—not to speak of what God has done! For two pins I'd knock their reverend pates together! . . . All this hair-splitting about texts! Why can't they agree to differ, like sensible people?

HOSIUS (*cautiously*)

Why indeed, Augustus? Unless the difference of opinion is really so fundamental that——

CONSTANTINE

It isn't. It's only some obscure metaphysical point—nothing but sophistry. All anybody wants is faith in God and Christ and the simple Gospel message. These theologians are getting swelled heads, that's what it is. They feel safe, they enjoy the Imperial favour, they're exempt from taxation, and instead of looking after the poor and converting the heathen, they start heresy-hunting and playing a sort of intellectual catch-as-catch-can to jockey one another out of benefices. I won't have it. It's got to stop. Hosius, you will start today and carry this letter to Alexandria. Oh! and you'd better have a look at the rest of the correspondence

[TOGI *hands* HOSIUS *a sheaf of papers.*

and mull it over with Lactantius while Togi makes his fair copy. (*He waves* HOSIUS *and* LACTANTIUS *to a seat.*) . . . All right, Togi, I'll see the suppliant in a moment. Give me a drink—a long one, just to calm me down. . . .

[TOGI *pours him a drink.*

I should like to smash something.

TOGI

Smash the amphora—it's only a second best one.

CONSTANTINE (*good-naturedly*)

If you're impudent, I shall send you back to Britain. (*He drinks.*) That's better. Now go and fetch the lady.

94

[*Exit* TOGI. CONSTANTINE *settles his dress and arranges himself in a suitable posture to receive the Suppliant.*)

LACTANTIUS (*in a low voice to* HOSIUS)

I'm afraid it will take more than an Imperial scolding to settle this.

HOSIUS

I'm sure it will. When the Easterns become obstinate in a matter of dogma, there's no shifting them.

LACTANTIUS

Sometimes they are over-subtle. But this looks like being a major issue. (*With a glance at* CONSTANTINE.) You have my sympathy.

HOSIUS

I shall need it.

[*Re-enter* TOGI, *ushering in* CONSTANTIA, *veiled.*

CONSTANTINE

Madam, what do you seek from Augustus?

[TOGI *goes back to his table and begins writing for dear life.*

CONSTANTIA (*embracing his knees*)

Mercy for the conquered.

CONSTANTINE

I have shown mercy before, Constantia.

CONSTANTIA

Blessed are the merciful. Blessed are they who forgive unto seventy times seven.

CONSTANTINE

Poor Constantia! I haven't done too well by my sisters, have I? First Anastasia, and now you, weeping at my feet because of the husbands I gave them to.

CONSTANTIA

You will not kill Licinius as you killed Bassianus?

95

CONSTANTINE

Bassianus was a traitor. Licinius was only unwise. We pulled together well enough for nine years—but he was always an ass yoked with a stallion.

CONSTANTIA

It was you who declared war.

CONSTANTINE

Technically, yes. But he asked for it by ill-treating Christ's people.

CONSTANTIA

You would have broken him in the end, Constantine, whatever he did. You always meant to be Emperor of the world.

CONSTANTINE

Did I? Perhaps I did. (*He raises her and puts back her veil.*) He has been kind to you?

CONSTANTIA

Always.

CONSTANTINE

I shall not trouble him, unless he troubles me. But he must not stay here in Nicomedia.

CONSTANTIA

He asks only his life, and permission to retire into some quiet spot with me and the children.

CONSTANTINE

It is granted. (*He leads her to a chair.*)

CONSTANTIA

And that you will spare his colleague Martinianus.

CONSTANTINE

H'm. I don't like the man. But since you ask it, it is granted. Only they must behave themselves. No rebellions, no conspiracies, no pleasant little plots to murder. Let them remember what happened to Maximian.

CONSTANTIA (*rather faintly*)

I will make that clear, Constantine.

96

Where is Licinius, Togi?

TOGI

Under house-arrest in his country villa, Augustus.

CONSTANTINE

Well, well, Constantia, bring him to dinner, and we will decide where is best for you to go. Be happy, my dear.

CONSTANTIA

Thank you, brother.

CONSTANTINE

Fausta arrived last night. She will be delighted to see you. . . . oh, by the way, this man Arius that all the trouble is about. Do you know anything of him?

[*This brings* HOSIUS *and* LACTANTIUS *back into the picture.*

CONSTANTIA

He came to Nicomedia in the summer to enlist the support of Bishop Eusebius. And he has been circularising all the churches in the East.

HOSIUS

Have you seen him, madam? What is he like?

CONSTANTIA

An elderly man, very tall and thin. He dresses like an ascetic, in the robe and short cloak of a philosopher. He has a great reputation for learning.

CONSTANTINE

One of your dry-as-dust, chop-logic pedants, eh?

TOGI

I am told, sir, that he has a polished tongue and that many devout ladies hear him gladly.

CONSTANTIA

He is certainly—impressive.

Dc   97

Togi

And that he has a knack of throwing his doctrines into verse, which can be set to popular tunes and sung in ale-houses.

Hosius

My dear Togius, how do you manage to pick up all this gossip?

Togi

Father, that is part of my secretarial duties. But, indeed, one can hardly set foot in the streets or get one's hair cut without hearing the opinions of this reverend excommunicate bawled or sung or suggested into one's ears.

Constantine

Do you mean to tell me that in this part of the world the common people are actually *interested* in theological controversy?

Togi

Oh, dear me, yes, sir. It's meat and drink to 'em. Better than a chariot-race. There's a good deal of fancy betting on Arius, but I think, sir, that most of the solid, knowledgeable people are putting their money on Alexander.

Constantine

Well, I don't know. A man who can get the women and the working classes into a state of excitement about philosophy must be a pretty fine publicist. Or, of course, a damned clever charlatan. Well, Hosius, it's your job to find out.

Hosius

Yes, Augustus.

Constantine

Off with you, then. Your horses are ordered, and your galley is waiting for you at the port of Byzantium. See what they're doing, tell them not to, and be back here with the next favourable wind.

[*Exeunt* Hosius, Lactantius *and* Constantia.

(*To* Togi) Is that letter finished? Give it to me to sign. . . . Bishops, indeed! I'll show them.

A.D. 324—*The following day.*   *Nicomedia: another room in the palace.*
($\frac{1}{2}$ *set B.*)

[HELENA *is sitting bolt upright at a table, silently spelling out an enormous volume of theology.* FAUSTA, *on a day-bed, is languidly trying the effect of a new set of jewellery, assisted by* BASSIANA MARCIA. *Between them,* CONSTANTIA *and* MATIBENA *are occupied with a strip of embroidery.*

FAUSTA

The diadem is pretty well. But the earrings are too long.

MARCIA

They are in the latest fashion, Augusta. All the Eastern noble-women are wearing them so.

FAUSTA

You don't think they look vulgar?

MARCIA

On a plebeian figure they would be excessive. But your ladyship's elegant neck and superb carriage set them off to perfection.

FAUSTA (*discontentedly*)

I don't know. What do you think, Constantia?

CONSTANTIA

The whole effect is imperial. They would be right for great occasions.

FAUSTA

That is what they are meant for. To uphold the dignity of the One Emperor and his belongings. . . . Do I look sufficiently impressive, Mamma?

HELENA

Why, yes, my dear. Constantine will be proud of you, as he always is.

FAUSTA

And the whole world will applaud his munificence. . . . Very well, Marcia, we will keep them. . . . What is that frightful great volume?

HELENA

It is a commentary on the Book of Proverbs.

FAUSTA

What in the world are you doing with that?

HELENA

Trying to understand it, my dear. Though I must say it's rather difficult, and I don't get on very fast.

CONSTANTIA

Are you interested in theological questions?

FAUSTA

Theology is the fashion here—like long ear-rings. My mother-in-law is a woman, you see. She likes to be fashionable, though she isn't interested in dress.

HELENA

Not at my age, daughter. But I am interested in anything that interests Constantine. And it looks as though he would have to be interested in the Book of Proverbs, poor dear. So I thought I would study it a little beforehand, so as to be ready to ask questions and look intelligent when the time comes.

FAUSTA

Constantine doesn't want one to be intelligent—only to look beautiful and agree with whatever he says and does.

HELENA

You are his wife, dear child. I am only his old mother, and can scarcely expect him to take notice of my looks. As for agreeing with him about everything—why should I? When he was little, I spanked him if he didn't behave. Now he is grown up, I retain my maternal privilege of scolding him when I think fit.

Matibena

So you say, my lady. But you always did spoil him and you always will.

Helena

I shall always be ready to listen and sympathise, which is what boys want of their mothers.

Constantia

And all men of their womenfolk.

Matibena

All the same, you didn't ought to encourage him, my lady—not to get arguing about the holy mysteries of God. How the Father begets the Son, indeed! That's not for the likes of us to pry into.

Fausta

I haven't an idea what it means, and I don't suppose anyone else has, either. . . . The bracelets, Marcia.

Matibena

Forgive us our trespasses and God be merciful to me a sinner—that's what he needs to learn. He never thinks of the blessed Lord that died to save us, except as an ally to win his battles for him. My old cat's as good a Christian as he is—mews when she's hungry and purrs when she's fed, and knows where her blessings come from.

Fausta

How dare you speak like that of the Emperor! If I were your mistress, I would have you whipped.

Helena

Your tongue runs away with you, Matibena. And I think it is the other way round. God needs His battles won, and has called Constantine to win them. All the same, there is truth in what you say—none of us feels the true love of God till we realise how wicked we are. (*Sighing.*) But you can't *teach* people that—they have to learn by experience.

Matibena

They won't learn it out of that big book. You'd better stop reading now, you'll tire your eyes out.

Well, perhaps I have done enough for today. Constantia, you have heard Arius and Bishop Eusebius discuss this question—do you remember what they said?

CONSTANTIA

A little. But they talked very learnedly. I was rather out of my depth.

HELENA

You must tell me about it. What a pity you and Licinius have to leave Nicomedia tomorrow. You could have helped me so much —if only it were possible for you to stay.

CONSTANTIA (*suddenly agitated*)

Never say that. Never think it. It is best that we should go, as far away as possible, and never be seen or heard of again. Thessalonica is not remote enough. We should go to a different world, if there were one, and begin a new life, without memories, and without temptations.

HELENA

My dear, do not speak so bitterly.

CONSTANTIA

I am not bitter. I only speak the truth. They that have once known power should never be left within sight or smell of what they have had and lost. They cannot be happy—and they are not safe. Fausta should know that.

FAUSTA

I have reason to know it.

CONSTANTIA

But you do not heed it.

FAUSTA

What do you mean?

MARCIA

Madam, if it is to me that you are referring, permit me to say that your hints are quite unjustified. To wait upon the Empress, whom I sincerely love, is happiness enough. The generosity of the Emperor, who bears me no ill-will for the fault of my misguided brother, is my safety, and in that I have implicit trust. You wrong the noble Constantine, madam, in supposing that he could be revengeful, and me too, if you suppose that I am not sensible of his magnanimity.

HELENA

Constantia, you have said too much—or too little.

MARCIA

Speak plainly, madam, do you accuse me of conspiracy? and with whom?

CONSTANTIA

I accuse no one—not even myself. But I say that I, and such as I, should be secluded—released into singleness of loyalty and dedicated to silence.

FAUSTA

Silence would certainly be better than this kind of talk. I think you must be hysterical. I hope so.

MATIBENA

Tired out, that's what it is. . . . You come along and lie down and let old Matibena give you some nice syrup of poppies, or you won't be fit to travel tomorrow. . . .

CONSTANTIA

I'm not a child. Leave me alone, Matibena.

[*Enter* CRISPUS.

CRISPUS

Aunt Constantia! Aunt Constantia! Come and see my new horse! (*He becomes aware of* HELENA's *presence.*) I'm sorry, Grand-mamma—shall I go out and come in again properly? (*He salutes her respectfully, and she smiles indulgently on him.*) . . . I say, Madam Mother, you look stupendous in that get-up—the Queen of Sheba isn't in it. . . . Do come, everybody! He's terrific! He says "Ha, Ha", among the trumpets, like the charger in *Job.*

HELENA (*thankful for this diversion*)

In a moment, dear boy. Fetch me my cloak, Matibena.

CONSTANTIA

He sounds wonderful. I'd love to see him.

FAUSTA

I'm afraid I'm not dressed for the stables. Another time.

CRISPUS (*shepherding off* HELENA, CONSTANTIA *and*
MATIBENA)

Two years old—black, without one white hair—I think I shall
call him Boanerges—by Melanippus out of Xantippe—you never
saw such a pair of shoulders. . . . (*And so on, with as much horse-
talk as is needed to take them all off.*)

FAUSTA (*sinking on the day-bed*)

Oh dear! I feel quite exhausted. . . . I think I have a headache
coming on.

MARCIA

No wonder, madam.

FAUSTA

Nobody has any consideration for my nerves. That was a most
unpleasant scene.

MARCIA

Perhaps, madam, it would be better for me to leave the court.
You ought not to be exposed to these insults for the sake of one
who is indebted to you for everything.

FAUSTA

Don't you desert me, Marcia. You're the only person who loves
me. That's why they want to get rid of you. Constantine's family
are impossible. They know I've no father or brother to stand up
for me. Constantine took care of that. And my own three beautiful
boys might as well not exist. It's all Crispus, Crispus, Crispus.
And he's so bad-mannered and noisy.

MARCIA

He is young, Augusta, and his victories at Byzantium and
Chrysopolis have over-excited him . . . Let me take off these
jewels, so that you can rest your head. (*Removing the diadem.*)

FAUSTA

Read to me, Marcia. Something to take my mind off.

MARCIA

From the Christian scriptures, Madam?

FAUSTA

No. . . . They are very improving, of course, and you must learn to be a Christian some day. But I wish the holy men had been inspired to write rather less abominable Greek. . . . Have you any classical poets?

MARCIA (*fetching out a roll*)

Perhaps you would like the *Hippolytus* of Euripides? It is a great masterpiece, and very exciting.

FAUSTA

Scarcely very appropriate. Isn't it about that silly woman Phaedra, who fell in love with her stepson?

MARCIA

And so turned his father's love against him that the young man was ruined and slain.

FAUSTA

A good conclusion. What sort of young man was the stepson?

MARCIA

A prig, madam, with no mind for anything but hunting and horses.

FAUSTA

No doubt he deserved what he got. Well—it will do as well as anything else. Begin.

MARCIA (*reading*)

"I am that goddess who is called the Cyprian,
Mighty on earth, not without name in Heaven. . . ."

SCENE 9

June, 324—*Nicomedia. As Sc.* 7

[CONSTANTINE, HELENA, FAUSTA, CRISPUS, HOSIUS, EUSEBIUS OF NICOMEDIA, LACTANTIUS.

CONSTANTINE

You say these churchmen cannot agree?

HOSIUS

They cannot agree, Augustus.

CONSTANTINE

And they will not submit?

HOSIUS

Until the question is decided, it is unfortunately not clear which party ought to submit.

CONSTANTINE

You mean to tell me that the question is of real importance?

HOSIUS

I am afraid it is, Augustus.

CONSTANTINE

I thought it was only a dispute about a text in *Proverbs*.

LACTANTIUS

Both sides try to use the text to back their arguments. But it is really a dispute about the Godhead of Christ.

CONSTANTINE

How can there be any dispute about that among Christians?

CRISPUS

Surely, believing that is just what makes one a Christian.

HOSIUS

Yes, Caesar, but you see——

CRISPUS

So the side which doesn't believe it must be wrong and they are the people who ought to submit.

HOSIUS

It is more complicated than that. Both Catholics and Arians would agree that Christ is true God, in relation to the whole created universe.

CRISPUS

Then where's the dispute?

106

Hosius

It is about His relation to God the Father. The Arians say that since He is begotten of the Father, He must be subsequent to the Father——

Constantine

That sounds reasonable enough. I begot Crispus—therefore Crispus must be subsequent to me.

Helena (*mildly*)

Constantine darling, you're not God.

[Fausta *laughs a little maliciously.*

Constantine

Please, Mother, don't try to be funny.

Lactantius

Forgive me, Augustus, what Madam Helena says is very just, though she has expressed it in rather a lively manner, as ladies will. She means that God, unlike even the greatest of created beings, is not subject to time.

Helena

Thank you, Lactantius—a highly ingenious commentary on a rather ambiguous text.

Hosius

Both text and commentary are exceedingly relevant. Do I understand Arius to say that the Son is a created being?

Eusebius

He uses some convincing arguments, quoting the eighth chapter of *Proverbs*, "God created Me in the beginning of His ways", which caused Origen to declare that the Son was a creature.

Helena

Yet; in the same context, Origen maintains that one cannot say of the Son that there was a time when He was not.

CRISPUS

Well done, Grandmamma! you've been reading your big book to some purpose.

HOSIUS

And St. John says that all things were created by the Son. So how can He be Himself a creature?

FAUSTA

Easily—like Plato's Demiurge.

[*This startles everybody.*

EUSEBIUS

I beg your pardon, madam?

CONSTANTINE

What do you know about Plato?

FAUSTA

I had *some* education before you married me. It's all quite simple, the way Eusebius puts it. God the Father is the same as Plato's One, who is just an abstract something-or-other; and the One somehow produced the Demiurge, and the Demiurge made the world. If you would only put it like that there wouldn't be any real quarrel between Platonists and Christians, and we could all worship the same God and get along very nicely.

CONSTANTINE

Fausta, please stop. You don't know what you are talking about.

FAUSTA

Of course, anything *I* say is bound to be idiotic.

LACTANTIUS

On the contrary, madam, you have put the case against Arius so forcibly that I can find nothing to add. If Christ is not true God equally with the Father, there is no essential difference between Christianity and pagan polytheism——

HOSIUS

I agree.

I deny that absolutely.

CONSTANTINE

Stop! You have convinced me that the question is important. It seems I shall have to turn theologian—if only to prevent my wife from relapsing into paganism. . . . Hosius, what do you suggest doing about it?

HOSIUS

There will have to be a council, I suppose.

CONSTANTINE

A church council—like the Council of Arles, that was supposed to be going to settle the Donatist dispute. And they will decide in favour of Arius or Alexander. And then the other party will appeal, and there will be another council and another decision, and then they will appeal again—just as they did before. What is the good of these councils where no decision is ever made final?

HOSIUS

With submission, Augustus. The Council of Arles came to a perfectly good and legal decision; and if your Augustitude would only have enforced their findings——

CONSTANTINE

No. That is impossible. If the Bishops had let *me* settle the question, as I offered to do, I could have enforced the findings of my own court. But they said the question was a matter for the churches only to decide—and if to decide, then to enforce. There cannot be two kinds of justice in one realm. I am emperor of all my people, within and without the Church, and the Imperial Courts must not be made an instrument for enforcing laws which they have not made. Church and State must decide as one and execute as one, sharing as one both the odium and the responsibility. Or they must separate—a church without material power and a state without religious opinions. But not half-and-half.

HOSIUS

I see.

LACTANTIUS

Then we must wait in patience upon the Holy Ghost.

In patience! If you would wait in patience you would set an
example of brotherly love to the whole world. But your patience
is schism, riot, open denunciation, excommunicated bishops flee-
ing from one see to another, and proclaiming their wrongs in
every Christian pulpit, so that the heathen laugh, and Church
and Empire are ashamed. . . . You praised God when I set the
Chi-Ro on the Imperial standards, when I privileged the worship
and priesthood of Christ, when I called Christians into my councils and put the reins of government into Christian hands. But
can't you see that all this makes a difference? When you were an
oppressed minority, you could quarrel among yourselves as much
as you liked—who cared? But now your light is set on a candle-
stick and cannot be hid. And if your light is darkness, how great
is that darkness!

HELENA

Oh, Constantine! that is only too true.

HOSIUS

Very aptly quoted, Augustus.

CONSTANTINE

Our Lord said to the Samaritan woman: "Ye worship ye know
not what; but we know whom we worship." *Do* you know whom
you worship? It would seem you do not. And it matters *now* that
you should. . . . What will you do? Go back to the obscurity from
which I raised you? and let the Holy Ghost speak once more by
the blood of the martyrs? Or accept for Christ the kingdom of
the world at my hands, and learn the responsibility that needs
must go with rule?

[*An awkward pause.*

HELENA

I have been afraid of this. For years I have seen it coming. Our
Lord said: "My kingdom is not of this world."

HOSIUS

True, madam. Yet, when He left His disciples, He put worldly
power in their charge, saying: "He that hath a purse, let him take
it; and he that hath no sword, let him sell his garment and buy
one."

He said also: "Preach the gospel to every creature." And when all are converted, there must needs be a Christian State.

CONSTANTINE (*drily*)

True. In that happy day there will be no poor pagan to take the burden and blame of office. Sirs, it is easy to be virtuous so long as you can criticise from outside; but it is not so easy when you have to wield power yourselves and take the consequences. . . . You do not seem eager to renounce power and take the consequences of *that*. Very well. . . . What is the seat of authority in the Church? By whom does the Holy Spirit speak?

LACTANTIUS

By the voice of the whole body of believers.

CONSTANTINE

In other words, by the general Synod—is that so? Then we shall call a Great Council of all the churches, East and West, to decide this important question. I shall call that Council myself—Christ's Emperor summoning Christ's Empire; and if any decision of that Council needs to be enforced, I will enforce it. The decision itself will be made, of course, by the Bishops—I have nothing to do with that. . . . In a year from now—that will give them time to assemble. We will do the thing handsomely, they shall travel at government expense.

HOSIUS

Shall they meet in Alexandria?

CONSTANTINE

No—there is too much local feeling. A neutral meeting-place. Not Rome—I do not want to go west. Not here—the city cannot accommodate such numbers. . . . How about Nicaea?—Yes, I like that. There is victory in the name. The logothetes shall go out to every corner of the Empire—and if we can set up truth victorious over heresy, fame shall account it the greatest of all the victories of Constantine.

ACT III

THE EMPIRE OF CHRIST

SCENE 1

May, 325—*Nicomedia. As Act II, Sc.* 9. (½ *set.*)

[CONSTANTINE, HOSIUS *and* LACTANTIUS *are sitting talking, after dinner with* ALEXANDER, *Bishop of Alexandria, and his Deacon,* ATHANASIUS, *a small, thin, energetic young man with pugnacious red hair.*

CONSTANTINE

Well, Bishop Alexander, I've been into this business as thoroughly as a rather busy layman can. I can certainly say I've heard both sides.

LACTANTIUS

Your Imperial Highness has been extraordinarily patient. Really, I sometimes thought we should never get Bishop Eusebius out of the Palace.

CONSTANTINE

Being the bishop on the spot, no doubt he feels it his duty to superintend my opinions. Though he was just as devoted to Licinius, who had no religious opinions at all. But he certainly made an enthusiastic Arian of my sister Constantia.

ALEXANDER

The man is a volcano of energy. I think he has circularised every bishop this side of the Adriatic. Though I haven't done badly myself. I have written at least seventy letters to the churches, with the aid of my energetic young deacon here.

CONSTANTINE

You and the Deacon Athanasius have put in some hard work on me, too, both on your first visit a year ago, and during these last few weeks. Then I've had Arius himself, who has even more staying-power than Eusebius of Nicomedia. Hosius has given me the Western point of view, and our learned Lactantius has furnished many colossal volumes of commentary, of which my Mother has laboriously made notes for my benefit. About two hundred bishops have sent me letters accusing one another of

112

heresy. And I have enjoyed a good deal of talk with Eusebius of Cæsarea—but since he is proposing to write my biography he is so anxious to say the polite thing that I can't discover which side he is on.

LACTANTIUS

A very able man, but a sadly slap-dash theologian.

CONSTANTINE

Anyhow, so far as my very amateur understanding goes, I am disposed to think that you are right, Alexander.

ALEXANDER

I am delighted to hear your Augustitude say so.

CONSTANTINE

Mind you, I may be prejudiced. I do find Arius rather a trying person.

HOSIUS

He has a reputation for charm, but his appearance is not calculated to adorn a court.

CONSTANTINE

I shouldn't mind that, though I wish he'd comb his hair. But he's so maddeningly superior. Every other sentence begins " It stands to reason "—as though nobody but an imbecile would want it explained at all. . . . Besides, I'm not sure that a thing like the nature of God *ought* to stand to reason in that obvious way. Surely one would *expect* it to be rather above one's head. . . . But perhaps I really am very stupid. Am I, Athanasius?

ATHANASIUS

Your Imperial Highness is not stupid at all. Far from it. You are not so familiar as we are with the technical jargon of theology, but when once it's put in plain language you have an excellent grasp of the matter.

CONSTANTINE

There! You see? Athanasius flatters my intelligence, so naturally I think he is right. Arius patronises me, so naturally I hope he is wrong.

ALEXANDER

I have always thought Arius the most tiresome type of intellectual.

HOSIUS

One does not feel in him any warm devotion to Our Lord—only an arid pleasure in a philosophical pattern.

CONSTANTINE

That's exactly what my mother says.

ALEXANDER

Indeed? Most women think the world of Arius.

CONSTANTINE

Most women enjoy being mystified—they find it very impressive. But I've never found my mother an easy person to impress—and it's not for want of trying. . . . Besides, she is really devout, which makes her good at seeing through other people's jargon.

LACTANTIUS (*mildly*)

It is a pity that we can't do without technical terms. But they do make for precision.

CONSTANTINE

Quite so. Which brings us back to this Council which starts next week. What you people want is to get this doctrine defined, one way or the other, and put into a creed. What I want is peace in the Church.

HOSIUS

We all want that, Augustus.

CONSTANTINE

Exactly. Well, it's up to you theologians to hammer out a definition. My business as chairman is, I take it, to steer the meeting towards agreement upon some elastic and shall we say oecumenical formula, which shall be correct from the doctrinal point of view and yet acceptable to all parties.

[*The others exchange glances.*

114

ALEXANDER (*with some hesitation*)

That, I think, Augustus, is what Arius and his party will want
you to do.

CONSTANTINE

Arius? Isn't it what we all want?

HOSIUS

Not altogether.

LACTANTIUS

That is what we have already; and it is over the interpretation
of the formula that all the disputes have arisen.

ALEXANDER

You see, Augustus, from what has emerged during the preliminary discussions which, as you know, have now been going
on for some weeks, it looks as though the Arian party will have
no chance at all of carrying their point. They have seriously
over-estimated their strength; the mind of the Church is against
them, and they are beginning to realise it. Consequently, when
they see they can't hope for an outright victory, their policy
will be to accept any phrase we propose, so that afterwards they
can interpret it in their own way, with every appearance of
orthodoxy.

HOSIUS

Exactly.

CONSTANTINE

But does it matter very much if they do? I mean, provided we
get a decent measure of outward conformity, can't we allow a
little latitude of interpretation on the subtler points? I do hate
all this straw-splitting and heresy-hunting, and bishops solemnly
excommunicating each other; it gets quite ludicrous—and it's
surely very uncharitable. There must be some kind of creed or
symbol, no doubt, laying down the basic lines of belief. But is it
necessary to be so rigidly literal? Isn't it true that the letter
killeth, but the spirit giveth life?

HOSIUS

Your Majesty's quotations are always so apt. In this case, unfortunately, the quarrel is precisely about the spirit in which the
letter is to be taken.

I am asking that it should be taken in a rather more liberal spirit.

[*The churchmen are depressed. It looks as though the Emperor were going to turn bad on them, and produce a nasty impasse.*

ATHANASIUS (*after a slight pause and with becoming modesty*)

If I may speak . . . Forgive me, Augustus; but would you display the same liberality of mind if the question were not of Christ's sovereignty, but of your own?

CONSTANTINE

What do you mean?

ATHANASIUS

Suppose there is a grammarian in your empire who says: " I am very willing, like everybody else, to call Constantine *Augustus* —for that word need after all mean only *dignified*, *noble*, or the like, and such he undoubtedly is. But that Constantine is our rightful emperor I do not and will not admit. Therefore, when I call him *Augustus* it is with the mental reservation that I understand the word in my own way and not the other, and this is the meaning that I shall teach to everyone who hears me lecture." Supposing this were to come to your august ears——

CONSTANTINE

I should have him arrested on the spot. . . . Is there such a man?

ATHANASIUS

Not that I know of. I only said " Suppose ".

CONSTANTINE

Well, you had me there. . . . You know, Alexander, this young friend of yours is an excellent teacher. That's why I like him so much better than Arius. He always finds some simple, handy illustration which makes the point ruthlessly clear. . . . Very well, I give in. My business as chairman is to guide the meeting towards some iron-clad expression which by no conceivable ingenuity can be twisted into meaning anything that Arius and his friends could possibly dream of accepting.

ALEXANDER

Precisely, Augustus.

LACTANTIUS

And such an expression is not very easily found.

HOSIUS

There is one which I think they would certainly boggle at. It's not new. It has been in use for some time in the Western Church.

LACTANTIUS

What is that?

ALEXANDER

I know what you are going to say.

HOSIUS

" Consubstantial with the Father."

ALEXANDER

I thought so. The Greek "homoöusios". The trouble is that in the East it has already been condemned.

LACTANTIUS

Every period has its own dangers. A word that was open to misconstruction in the last century may be harmless and even salutary now. What do you think, Athanasius?

ATHANASIUS

Sir, I think words matter little, provided the intention is right. It is better that people should use different words and mean the same thing than that they should use the same words with contradictory meanings. And it is quite certain that nobody could use the word " homoöusios " or " consubstantialis " and mean what Arius means. So that, provided the distinction of the Son's Person is safeguarded, I can see no objection to the phrase.

ALEXANDER

If only the Council can be got to accept it.

HOSIUS

You can count on the support of the West.

Unfortunately, my dear Hosius, the West is going to be very poorly represented. The Bishop of Rome has not troubled to come——

HOSIUS

He is really far too old. He has sent two representatives.

CONSTANTINE

The fact remains that out of three-hundred-odd delegates there will be only seven Western bishops, including yourself, Hosius.

HOSIUS (*chagrined*)

Is that all?

ALEXANDER

I fear the West is not very theologically minded.

CONSTANTINE (*hastily*)

Well, we must do our best. . . . Write the word down for me, Athanasius, and if necessary I will put it from the chair. . . . You know, reverend Fathers, it looks as though this Council will reach its decision, not so much by inspiration of the Holy Ghost as by your scholarship and polemical training, my practical statesmanship, and a good deal of what, in another context, I should be inclined to call lobbying.

ALEXANDER

Neither you nor we, Augustus, can dictate to the Holy Ghost. We are not the Church, we are only the gifts of the Church, and He who bestowed the gifts will use them as it seems good to Him, and will speak with the voice of the Church. The decision will not rest with Arius, nor with me—no, nor with the Emperor of the world, but with the lovers of Christ gathered from every land. Potamon of Heraclea and James of Nisibis have come from the deserts, and Spiridion the shepherd-bishop of Cyprus from following his flocks and herds. Theophilus the Goth and Cathirius from the Bosphorus heard the call among the barbarians; Jerusalem and Antioch have sent their bishops from streets which once knew the tread of Christ and His Apostles. There will be confessors and martyrs among us—Paphnutius of the Thebaid, who was blinded and mutilated under Diocletian, and Paul of Neocaesarea, whose hands were burned with hot irons for the sake of Christ. Our little wisdoms are not alone, being compassed about with so great a cloud of witnesses, and supported by the prayers of the saints. Do you think that emperors and priests make history? No, but the Lord of history, who was content to be condemned by the High Priest and crucified by the Imperial Procurator that He might mould the history of the world to the pattern He had ordained from the beginning.

CONSTANTINE

I stand rebuked, Alexander.

LACTANTIUS

"To the Jews a scandal, and to the Greeks foolishness"—and even to Christians, the follies of the faithful are apt to be disconcerting.

CONSTANTINE

Well, tomorrow we start for Nicaea, where I shall hope to hear nothing but wisdom. Let us drink to the good outcome of the Council.

SCENE 2

May, 325. A street in Nicaea. (Before tabs.)

[A FISHMONGER'S BOY *enters and passes across the stage.*

FISHMONGER'S BOY (*singing shrilly*)

Arius of Alexandria, I'm the talk of all the town,
Friend of saints, elect of Heaven, filled with learning and renown:
If you want the Logos-doctrine, I can serve it hot and hot——

[*Exit* FISHMONGER'S BOY *singing. Tabs open.*

SCENE 3

May 325—Nicaea: a barber's shop. (½ set A.)

[*There are three* BARBERS (PHILO, STEPHEN, *and* EUTYCHUS) *and a* BOY, *trying to attend to five customers at once. The three chairs are at the moment occupied by an enthusiastic young Christian called* THEOPHILUS; *his friend, a Christian* DEACON, *and a middle-aged man in the dress of a* PHILOSOPHER. *Standing or sitting on a bench, waiting for attention, are an old and peppery retired* GENERAL *and a* GENTLEMAN *of Gnostic leanings and fashionable appearance.*

FISHERMAN'S BOY (*passes, singing off*)

God begat Him, and before He was begotten, He was not.

Head-Barber (Philo) (*to* Deacon)

A trifle shorter above the ears, sir? Boy, bring a mirror.

2nd Barber (Stephen) (*releasing* Theophilus)

Thank you, sir. Any pomade today, sir? No, sir. Thank you, sir. That will be twelve asses, sir. Thank you, sir. (*Receiving tip*) Thank you very much, sir. Good day, sir.

Deacon

Wait for me, Theophilus.

Theophilus

Rather.

Gentleman (*whisking ahead of* General *into* Theophilus' vacant chair)

Hair-cut and shave and look sharp about it.

General

How much longer have I got to wait?

Stephen

Boy! get this razor stropped. Hurry!

Philo

Very sorry, General. . . . Eutychus! . . . Very busy today, General. . . . Eutychus, take the noble General next.

Eutychus

Boy! the mirror!

Stephen

Boy! boy, my scissors! . . . (*To* Gentleman) Your first visit to Nicaea, sir?

Gentleman

Yes, and I don't mind if it's my last. Nothing fit to eat in the inns, and the prices are appalling.

Stephen

Town's very full, sir, because of the Council next week. Strangers arriving every day.

You're telling me. Is the Emperor here?

STEPHEN

Since Monday, sir. And the Empress and Lady Helena are expected today.

PHILO

Boy! bring the basin!

THEOPHILUS (*to* DEACON)

Hear that, Johannes? We must see the Lady Helena. (*Expansively*) She's a great patroness of our church. So pious and generous.

STEPHEN

Boy! hurry up with that razor!

THEOPHILUS

They say it was she made the Emperor a Christian.

GENERAL

T'scha! don't you believe it! She started life as a barmaid. When I was in Drepanum, in old Diocletian's days——

[BOY *falls over his feet.*

Damn it, boy!

Why don't you look where you're going?

PHILO

Boy! boy! a basin and some more soap! (*He starts to shave* DEACON.)

FISHMONGER'S BOY (*Singing off*)

If you want the Logos-doctrine—(*Breaks off to cry*) Fish! Fish! Fine fresh fish!

EUTYCHUS

Speaking as a philosopher, sir, have you any opinion upon this question about the Logos?

PHILOSOPHER

Oh, that? Arius is quite right, of course. The Logos, or the Word, or the Son as the Christians call Him, corresponds to the First Aeon in Plotinus, and is an emanation of the——

Sir, I take issue with you there. The God of the Christians is not a Monad, but a Triad—three Gods conjoined; the Father, the Son, and the Sophia or Wisdom, which is the female principle of the universe, and the——

THEOPHILUS

No, no, no! There is one God only and no female principle—is there, Johannes?

DEACON

Of course not—what a blasphemous idea! Owch! (*The soap goes into his mouth.*)

PHILO

Very sorry, sir. Boy! bring a towel.

EUTYCHUS

Getting a little thin on top, sir. May I recommend a bottle of our Samson Hair-Restorer?

PHILOSOPHER

No, thank you. Neither do I want face-cream, or perfume, or massage——

[*Enter* TOGI.

EUTYCHUS

Lotions, unguents, depilatories——

PHILOSOPHER

Nothing more, thank you. (*Rising*) How much is that? (*Gives money.*)

TOGI (*darting into* PHILOSOPHER'S *chair, again frustrating* GENERAL)

Shave, Eutychus, and see that your razor is sharp this time.

GENERAL

Upon my word, sir! Where are your manners? Can't you take your turn like other people? . . . Hi, Philo! Philo! You told him to take me next.

PHILO

Extremely sorry, General. In a moment, General. (*In his ear*) Very important official, General.

122

Damn your important officials!

[DEACON *rises to go.*

PHILO

Boy! this gentleman's cloak.

DEACON (*buttonholing* PHILOSOPHER *on his way out*)

Are you interested in Christian philosophy, sir? That gentleman has got it all wrong. There is one God only, the Father and Maker of all things——

THEOPHILUS

—and His Son, Jesus Christ is one with Him——

DEACON

—as He says in the tenth of St. John: "I and My Father are one"——

THEOPHILUS

—and the Holy Ghost is one with the Father and the Son——

DEACON

—as it says in St. John's First Epistle——

GENTLEMAN

That makes three. Three into one won't go.

STEPHEN

Very true, sir. That's what I always say. You can't go behind mathematics. And then there's the biological aspect. A son can't be as old as his father—very funny world if he could—Friction, sir? Thank you, sir. . . . We come back to the old problem of the hen and the egg.

THEOPHILUS (*indignantly*)

Don't be flippant, fellow.

PHILO

Very interesting, sir, these theological conundrums.

GENERAL

Curse your conundrums! Worship as the Emperor tells you, that's my motto, and see that your boots are clean for church parade.

(*To* Deacon) If you're going, sir, for heaven's sake go, and make room for your elders. (*He pushes into* Deacon's *chair.*)

DEACON (*to* GENTLEMAN)

And as for your female principle, sir, in the Deity, sir——

GENTLEMAN

Oh, I'm all for the female principle—in everything.

[STEPHEN *sniggers.*

GENERAL

They say this fellow Arius goes about with a following of seven hundred dedicated virgins.

GENTLEMAN

What a man!

DEACON

If you think it a proper subject for dirty jokes, sir——

FISHMONGER'S BOY (*singing off*)

God begat Him, and before He was begotten He was not.

LOUD MALE VOICE (*interrupting and singing off*)

Ladies many and various
Run after Father Arius—
He knows what's what and he serves it hot—
How many sons has Arius got?

ANOTHER VOICE (*off*)

Gertcha! (*Followed by sounds of a scuffle.*)

THEOPHILUS (*rushing to door*)

How disgusting!

[*The door opens suddenly in his face, to admit an excessively hairy person, who looks like John the Baptist, but is in fact* JAMES, *Bishop of Nisibis.*

JAMES

Peace be unto you! Peace be unto you!

Good God!

PHILO (*recovering himself*)

Certainly, sir. Trim and shave, sir?

BOY (*rushing up with enormous shears*)

Scissors, sir?

[PHILO *cuffs him over the ears.*

JAMES

Has anybody seen my donkey?

PHILOSOPHER

Here are two donkeys, good man—— (*Indicating* DEACON *and* THEOPHILUS.)

GENTLEMAN

Who are asses enough to believe that three equals one.

DEACON

Sir, I am a churchman——

THEOPHILUS

I'm a peaceful man as a rule——

DEACON

But I resent your impertinence——

THEOPHILUS

But I won't be called names by anybody——

JAMES

Someone has stolen my donkey.

GENERAL

Disgraceful! disgraceful!

JAMES

I left her outside this door.

PHILO

You should go to the magistrate.

BOY (*shouting at door*)

Thieves! thieves! police! Balaam's lost his ass!

THEOPHILUS

. . . ashamed of yourself at your age . . .

GENTLEMAN

. . . airing your silly opinions in public . . .

DEACON

. . . encouraging lewd talk among slaves and shopkeepers . . .

PHILOSOPHER

. . . barbarian ignorance and crass superstition . . .

JAMES

My donkey! My donkey!—she is church property!

PHILO (*trying to push him out*)

See here, my fine fellow——

JAMES (*in a despairing shriek*)

I am the Bishop of Nisibis.

TOGI

Oh lord! . . . Stop that noise, you fools! . . . There, there,
reverend father! it shall be seen to . . . I'll see to it myself.

GENTLEMAN (*leaping up*)

Who are you calling a fool?

JAMES (*struggling across to* TOGI)

Thank you, thank you! I only went into church to say my
prayers——

GENTLEMAN

Out of the way, Nebuchadnezzar! (*Pushing him.*)

GENERAL (*catching his arm*)

Stop that, you! What the blazes are we coming to! Barbers wrangling about God, donkeys stolen in broad daylight, town full of riff-raff (*he shakes the* GENTLEMAN *off into the arms of* THEOPHILUS), and that old trollop Helena flaunting about in the purple——

TOGI (*bouncing up with his face all over soap*)

Damn you! what do you mean by that?

GENTLEMAN

Blast you, let go!

DEACON

. . . old enough to know better . . .

THEOPHILUS

. . . teach you where to get off . . .

PHILOSOPHER

. . . don't threaten me, young man! . . .

BARBERS

Gentlemen, gentlemen!

GENERAL

. . . forty years back, served me with drinks at Drepanum——

TOGI

That's a lie!

GENERAL

. . . and I don't care if you are the Emperor's favourite slave——

BISHOP (*clinging to* TOGI)

My donkey! my donkey!

TOGI

That's another lie. I'm as free born as you are!

THEOPHILUS

I'm not standing any more of this!

127

Gentlemen, for pity's sake!

[*A crowd begins to collect at the door.*

TOGI

The Lady Helena is a princess of Britain——

GENERAL

Britain my foot! Nothing but a barmaid from Bithynia.

TOGI

. . . wife to the Emperor Constantius . . .

GENERAL

Constantius's wench, and a pretty wench too.

GENTLEMAN (*hitting* THEOPHILUS)

And to hell with you and your theology!

TOGI (*trying to free himself from* BISHOP *and* EUTYCHUS)

Take that back!

[*The* GENERAL *retreats slightly.*

THEOPHILUS

. . . and take that!

[*He knocks the* GENTLEMAN *flying against* STEPHEN *who staggers against the* GENERAL'S *back, and falls heavily into a pile of brass basins. The* GENERAL, *taking this for an assault in the rear, swings round and attacks the* PHILOSOPHER.

[*General scrimmage.*

BARBERS AND BOY

Help! murder! police!

BISHOP

My donkey! my donkey!

THEOPHILUS (*struggling in the arms of* PHILO)

Let 'em all come!

DEACON

Heretics! atheists!

GENTLEMAN

I'll break your head for that!

GENERAL (*seizing* PHILOSOPHER *by the beard*)

Get out, you old goat.

TOGI

The Emperor shall hear of this..

[*At this point, the Police, represented by a number of* SOLDIERS, *arrive on the scene, pushing through the* CROWD, *which is now shouting impartially for Arius, Alexander, Constantine, and any other names which occur to them—or just shouting. The scene closes in a happy confusion.*

SCENE 4

[*May 20th, 325—Nicaea: an anteroom to the council-chamber. (Before tabs.)*

[*Throughout this scene, the various* BISHOPS *whose names occur in the cast-list drift on to the stage from either side, and hang about in little groups, until it is time for them to go off P.S. in order to enter the chamber and be announced by the* USHER. *The* BISHOPS, *whose names are announced, but do not appear in the cast-list, are supposed to be entering the Chamber from another ante-room situated somewhere off-stage.*

USHER'S VOICE (*off-stage*)

Marcellus, Bishop of Ancyra . . . Leontius, Bishop of Caesarea in Cappadocia; Maris, Bishop of Chalcedon . . . Narcissus, Bishop of Neronias. . . .

HOSIUS (*who comes on early, and seems to have constituted himself a kind of master of the ceremonies*)

Well, Theognis; Nicaea is affording us magnificent hospitality.

THEOGNIS OF NICAEA

It is a great occasion.

HOSIUS

The name of your bishopric will certainly go down to history. The first Oecumenical Synod of the whole Church, East and West!

THEOGNIS

I only wish we had more delegates from the West.

Ec

HOSIUS (*a little shortly, for he is sensitive on this point*)

So do I, but it can't be helped.. . . . Ah, Theophilus! You must find this climate a great change from your frozen North.

THEOPHILUS OF PITYONTES

Oh, the sun shines sometimes even in the Caucasus.

HOSIUS

I had imagined it was all ice. . . .

USHER (*off*)

Paulinus, Bishop of Tyre . . . Hypatius, Bishop of Gangra. . . .

HOSIUS

Good day, James of Nisibis. . . . Did you ever find your donkey?

JAMES OF NISIBIS

No, but the Emperor has given me a new one, twice so handsome. . . . Peace be to you, Brother Spiridion. This palace is full of pomps and vanities.

SPIRIDION OF CYPRUS

I do not know where I am. . . .

USHER (*off*)

Aetius, Bishop of Lydda. . . .

SPIRIDION

Sometimes I am homesick for the bleatings of my lambs. But it is all most beautiful.

USHER (*off*)

Cathirius, Bishop of the Bosphorus . . . Gregory, Bishop of Berytus. . . .

HOSIUS

Eustathius! Eustathius of Antioch!

USHER (*off*)

Menophantes, Bishop of Ephesus. . . .

130

HOSIUS

You will be President of the Council, of course, Eustathius. . . .
Yes, yes—the seniority of your see, and the fact that you pre-
sided at Ancyra and Antioch—who so fitting? It is the wish
of Augustus.

EUSTATHIUS

In that case, of course.

HOSIUS

But—I hope you will not mind—he is anxious that I should
sit on his other side, to prompt him about procedure and so
on. He is used to me, you know. You see no objection?

EUSTATHIUS

Surely not. . . . Arius is here, I see. . . . Over there, with Secundus
of Ptolemais. . . .

USHER (*off*)

James, Bishop of Nisibis; Spiridion, Bishop of Cyprus. . . .
Caecilian, Bishop of Carthage. . . .

HOSIUS

Oh, yes—I wanted to ask you—do we let him put his own case
or confine the discussion to the bishops—as would be more
strictly correct?

EUSTATHIUS

I see no reason why we should not call on him to speak—if that
seems desirable.

HOSIUS

We-ell! If we don't, he will always complain that he never had
a fair hearing; and if we do—his eloquence may not prove
irresistible. . . . He irritates Augustus.

EUSTATHIUS

Does he? H'm! . . . I think we should get, say, Eusebius of
Nicomedia to put the case formally, and then perhaps allow
Arius to join in the open discussion.

USHER (*off*)

Theodotus, Bishop of Laodicea. . . . John, Metropolitan Bishop
of India. . . .

HOSIUS

Thank you, yes, that is a good idea.

EUSTATHIUS

Look! there is dear old Paphnutius! I think it is wonderful of him to have travelled all this way from the Thebaid, at his age, and maimed as he is. . . . Who is that with him? He too must be one of the martyrs.

HOSIUS

That is Paul of Neocaesarea—his hands are completely paralysed —burned with hot irons in the persecutions. . . . Excuse me, I must speak to Eusebius of Nicomedia.

USHER (*off*)

Theophilus, Bishop of Pityontes. . . . Patrophilus, Bishop of Scythopolis. . . . Macarius, Bishop of Jerusalem. . . .

AMPHION OF EPIPHANIA (*to* PAPHNUTIUS *and* PAUL)

Welcome, welcome, dear fellow-witnesses of Christ.

PAPHNUTIUS

Amphion of Epiphania! (*They embrace.*) We met last in the prison-house of Diocletian.

PAUL (*embracing Amphion*)

You have only just arrived?

AMPHION

I was delayed by sickness. But I thank our Saviour, I have got here in time. We are to bear witness again, it seems.

PAUL

But how differently!

PAPHNUTIUS

Blessed be God, who has given us a ruler, like David, after His own heart!

USHER (*off*)

Nicasias, Bishop of Die. . . . Theonas, Bishop of Marmarica. . . . Potamon, Bishop of Heraclea. . . .

EUSEBIUS OF NICOMEDIA

Arius. . . . It has all been arranged with Eustathius of Antioch. You are to be called on to speak.

ARIUS

Good. That is as it should be. After all, it stands to reason that since the cause is mine, I should be allowed to plead it.

SECUNDUS

Yes, indeed.

EUSEBIUS OF NICOMEDIA

But even with the advantage of your eloquence, we may fail to carry the day.

ARIUS

I shouldn't wonder. Look at some of my spiritual superiors! Crazy fanatics out of the desert—Spiridion there, babbling of tegs and ewes—and that extraordinary-looking Goth in the barbarian trousers—their votes count as much as your own. I am more afraid of them than of Alexander and that young cockerel who does all his crowing for him.

EUSEBIUS OF CAESAREA

I fancy you will have to be content with a compromise. I shall put forward as a basis for discussion the symbol we use in our own diocese. It is entirely non-committal.

THEOGNIS

Eusebius of Caesarea is quite right. All we really need is to have the thing left an open question.

EUSEBIUS OF CAESAREA

They will suggest modifications, of course.

EUSEBIUS OF NICOMEDIA

It doesn't matter, provided we accept any formula they agree to adopt.

ARIUS

Yes. There is no scriptural phrase which is not susceptible of a rational interpretation; and they will scarcely dare to suggest anything that is not in the Scriptures.

That old dotard Paphnutius and his fellow-simpletons will see
to that.

ARIUS

True—they have their uses after all.

THEOGNIS

The Emperor, of course, is a dark horse.

ARIUS

Oh, I think I've got the Emperor taped. It stands to reason——

EUSEBIUS OF CAESAREA

All *he* wants is to keep things quiet.

USHER (*off*)

The Presbyters Victor and Vincent, delegates of the Bishop of
Rome. . . .

THEOGNIS (*to* ARIUS)

And once you have all subscribed to their agreed formula, they
will be obliged to readmit you to communion. . . .

EUSEBIUS OF NICOMEDIA

And that, after all, is what we are really here for. . . . (*He looks
round and sees that the stage is empty.*) Shall we go in?

USHER (*off*)

Nicholas, Bishop of Myra. . . . Athanasius, Bishop of Anazarbus. . . .

[*The traverse opens.*

SCENE 5

[*Continuous with the preceding. The stage shows the council-chamber,
with seats along the sides running off diagonally P.S.; and a gilded
chair for* CONSTANTINE *up R. centre. Between the rows of seats, down-
stage, stands a low table, bearing a copy of the Gospels, open at the first
chapter of St. John. The Bishops who have been previously announced are
already in their places; the rest are entering P.S. downstage corner.*

Alexander, Bishop of Alexandria, and Athanasius his Deacon.
. . . Paphnutius, Bishop of the Thebaid . . . Paul, Bishop of
Neocaesarea in Pontus. . . . Amphion, Bishop of Epiphania. . . .
Eusebius, Bishop of Nicomedia. . . . Eusebius, Bishop of Caesarea
in Palestine. . . . Secundus, Bishop of Ptolemais and the
Presbyter Arius. . . . Theognis, Bishop of Nicaea. . . . Eustathius,
Bishop of Antioch. . . . Hosius, Bishop of Cordova. . . .

[EUSTATHIUS *takes his seat on the right of the Emperor's chair;*
HOSIUS *on the left, and next him* EUSEBIUS OF NICOMEDIA *and* EUSE-
BIUS OF CAESAREA. *About half-way down on the up-stage side of the
room is* ALEXANDER, *with* ATHANASIUS *on a low stool at his feet.
On the down-stage side, at front-stage, is a group of Arians, including*
ARIUS *himself,* THEOGNIS, SECUNDUS *and* THEONAS. *A* DEACON *acts
as secretary.*

*The Assembly being seated, there is a hush of expectation. A trumpet
sounds, and all heads are turned towards the door. Tramp of armed men off
P.S.*

PAPHNUTIUS

Is he coming?

NICHOLAS

I think so.

[*Tramp of* SOLDIERS *stops, off.*

SPIRIDION

Yes—the doors are opening——

[*A prolonged "Ah!" of astonishment and admiration goes up from the
assembled* BISHOPS, *beginning off-stage, and coming up the room, and the*
COUNCIL *rise to their feet,* NICHOLAS *and* SPIRIDION *assisting* PAPHNU-
TIUS *to rise, and* THEOPHILUS *and* ATHANASIUS *assisting* PAUL. *This
movement should also come up the room, and, after a sufficient time for
him to have passed between the double row of the remaining* 300 BISHOPS
off-stage:

Enter CONSTANTINE, *wearing the diadem and the Imperial purple,
followed by a few Officers of his Household, and* TOGI *and*
LACTANTIUS. CONSTANTINE *passes up the room to his seat, "with a
modest aspect and a blush upon his cheek", and stands there while the
Household take their places behind him.*

THEOPHILUS (*whispering*)

Oh, how beautiful!

POTAMON (*whispering*)

Like a shining angel of God.

PAUL (*whispering*)

He has been a blessed angel to the Church.

[*All the simpler* BISHOPS *are greatly affected, especially the Martyrs.*

CONSTANTINE

Most reverend Fathers, have I your permission to be seated?

EUSTATHIUS

Sir, it is for you——

CONSTANTINE

No, no.

[*After a little preliminary bowing and politeness,* CONSTANTINE *and the* BISHOPS *at the upper end of the room sit down, and the rest of the* COUNCIL *follow their example.* CONSTANTINE *signs to* EUSTATHIUS *to proceed.*

EUSTATHIUS (*rising*)

Your Imperial Majesty—Reverend Fathers: It is scarcely necessary for me to say with what emotions we find ourselves gathered here in this, the first Great Synod of the whole Eastern and Western Church, beneath the protection of Your Imperial Majesty, and honoured by your gracious presence. What the Church suffered in the past, Your Majesty well knows, and we all can bear witness; indeed, there are some among us who even today bear visibly in their bodies the marks of the Lord Christ. It was Your Majesty who, openly confessing Jesus Christ and Him crucified, and bearing His most holy Name upon your victorious banners, overthrew the tyrant Licinius and the other enemies of the Church, and freed us from terror and persecution; it is you that, honouring the servants of Christ and raising His people from the dust, have brought all the kingdoms of the world to acknowledge the sway of the King of Kings. It is you that have convened us to this most happy assembly; and it is for us to welcome Your Imperial Majesty, most humbly and gratefully as subjects, and may we say, as the unworthy representatives of Our Lord in His Church, most lovingly, to the United Council of Christendom. (*He resumes his seat amid confirmatory applause.*)

136

Bishop Eustathius and Most Reverend Fathers of the Church. I thank you from my heart for your welcome, and for your permission to me, a humble layman, to be present at your sacred counsels.

My friends, it has been my most fervent desire to see you thus gathered, and now my wish has come true. I give thanks before you all to the Ruler of the Universe, who, after all His other blessings, has vouchsafed to me this yet greater boon of beholding you all assembled in one common thought of concord. May no mischievous enemy disturb our present peace; and since, through the power of God our Saviour, the tyrants who set themselves up against God have disappeared, let no malicious spirit expose the Divine Law to blasphemies. To me, your fellow-servant, any dissension within the Church appears a thing as dreadful as war, and perhaps—I speak as a soldier—more difficult to bring to an end. I have been deeply pained, during these last few months, to receive a great number of letters containing accusations made by Christian bishops against their brother-bishops.

[TOGI *hands him a packet of papers, and signs to those behind the chair. A brazier is brought in.*

These, as you see, I have made into one great packet and sealed from all eyes—and in your presence I dispose of them thus. (*He drops the packet into the brazier.*) I beseech you, as your fellow-servant, to put aside all personal enmities, remembering the duty laid upon us all to forgive even as we would be forgiven. And I pray that the Holy Spirit may guide your counsels to a right and harmonious issue.

[*The brazier is carried out. The* BISHOPS *murmur applause, and some register a little confusion under this rebuke.*

Meanwhile CONSTANTINE *confers for a moment with* EUSTATHIUS, *and turns to speak to* HOSIUS, *who rises.*

HOSIUS

In the name of the Father and of the Son and of the Holy Ghost.

[*All rise.*

Almighty God, Father of Heaven, send down, we beseech Thee, Thy blessing upon this our undertaking. Blessed Lord Jesus Christ, Word of God, Son of the Father, assist us with Thy wisdom. Holy Spirit of God, be present with us and guide us into all truth. Amen.

[*All sit.*

EUSTATHIUS (*rising*)

Brothers in Christ: a number of questions of varying importance have, as you know, been referred to this Council for discussion and settlement. There is, first, the dispute concerning the Deity of the Son of God, which may call for the insertion of a more precise defining clause in the Baptismal Symbol of the Churches. There is the dispute in Egypt about the proper treatment of lapsed Christians. There is the question about the correct date for keeping the Festival of Easter, and there are various minor problems of ecclesiastical discipline, which you will find listed on the agenda papers.

I propose that we should take these items in the order that I have named, beginning with the question about Our Lord's Godhead, which is clearly the most important, since it is a matter of doctrine, and concerns the very foundations of our most holy Faith. I call upon the Bishop of Alexandria, in whose diocese the dispute first arose, to open the debate. (*He sits down. Each* BISHOP *rises when his turn is to speak, and sits when he has finished, and so throughout, unless otherwise indicated.*)

ALEXANDER

Brethren, it is now something over two years since my attention was drawn to a sermon preached in my own diocese by the Presbyter Arius, who, taking as his text the 22nd verse of the eighth chapter of *Proverbs*, appeared to deny the true Godhead of Our Lord Jesus Christ. Sending for him to rebuke what I took to be some accidental indiscretion or clumsiness of phrasing, I found that he actually meant what he said, and was prepared to support his position by arguments. After two debates, in which Arius expressed his opinions in a form yet more extreme, I thought it advisable to summon an episcopal council from the adjoining provinces. About a hundred bishops attended. All, with the exception of the Bishops of Ptolemais and Marmarica —who, I see, are here today—united in condemning the doctrine of Arius as heretical, and the council proceeded to excommunicate and banish him together with certain of his adherents. I hoped the matter would end there. But Arius, remaining obdurate, fled to Nicomedia——

138

I did not flee—I went.

ALEXANDER

He went, then, to Nicomedia, where he obtained the support of Bishop Eusebius, who at once initiated a campaign on his behalf, alleging that he had been subjected to persecution and arbitrary banishment. This obliged me to circularise my brethren of the Eastern Province, to acquaint them with the sentence passed by my council. The controversy then became widespread and embittered, so that our gracious Augustus, on his triumphal entry into Nicomedia, was distressed and angered by the scandal it provoked, and sent letters to Alexandria, urging us to compose our differences. But it seemed to us that in this matter we ought to seek the mind of the whole Church, under the guidance of the Holy Ghost; to whose decision we now submit ourselves, well knowing that where two or three are gathered together in Christ's name, He is in the midst of them and opens unto them by His Spirit the things concerning Himself.

EUSTATHIUS

I call upon the Bishop of Nicomedia to explain to the Council precisely what this doctrine is for which Arius was condemned, but which he himself is said to support.

EUSEBIUS OF NICOMEDIA

I think I cannot do better, at this point, than to read you the letter written to me by the Presbyter Arius after his expulsion from Alexandria. He says: " I think it proper and necessary to inform you that the Bishop of Alexandria is assaulting and persecuting us and employing every device against us, to the point of expelling us from the city, because we repudiate the doctrine he publicly preaches. He says: ' Always God, always the Son; at the same time the Father and the Son. The Son coexists ingenerately with God; He is ever begotten, He is ingenerately begotten. Neither in thought nor by a single moment does God precede the Son. The Son is as the Father Himself.' With this"
—the writer goes on—"we cannot agree. And when your brother Eusebius of Caesarea, and Theodotus and Paulinus and in fact all the Bishops of the East, declare that God is without beginning pre-existent to the Son, they have become anathema.

"We cannot endure to hear these blasphemies, though the

heretics should threaten us with a thousand deaths. What we say and believe we have taught and still teach: that the Son is not ingenerate or a part of the ingenerate in any way; nor yet formed from any underlying matter. But that He came into being by God's will and council before all times and ages, fully God, only-begotten and unchangeable; and before He was begotten, or created, or determined or founded, He did not exist, for He was not ingenerate. We are persecuted for saying: ' The Son has a beginning, God is without beginning.' For this—and because we said that because the Son was neither a part of God nor formed out of matter, therefore He was produced out of nothing. These are the grounds of our persecution.''

There the letter ends. I have nothing to add, except that the opinions of Arius seem to me to be founded in reason and sustained by many passages in Holy Writ.

EUSTATHIUS

The debate is now open.

EUSEBIUS OF CAESAREA

Since my name has been mentioned, may I say at once, that I do not associate myself with the doctrine of Arius. I keep an open mind in the matter. When my attention was drawn to it, I considered that it was worth while looking into, and should not be lightly condemned, and passed a resolution urging the Bishop of Alexandria, on the one hand, to restore Arius to communion and to his parish church, and Arius, on the other hand, to submit himself to his bishop, as a matter of discipline, and to seek reconciliation with him.

ALEXANDER

Instead of which, Arius and his friends made themselves as obnoxious as possible, holding unauthorised conventicles, night and day, provoking riots, instigating various elderly ladies to bring lawsuits against me, and allowing bands of disorderly young women to make demonstrations in the streets, to the grave discredit of the Christian religion.

AMPHION

May I add that I was greatly shocked, on arriving in Nicaea, to hear some very vulgar songs——.

Please let us keep to the point. We are at present concerned with doctrine.

[JOHN OF INDIA *and* NICHOLAS OF MYRA *rise together.*

John of India.

JOHN

I should like to ask what precise significance we are to attach to the word " ingenerate ", which is rather loosely used in the letter under discussion.

EUSEBIUS OF NICOMEDIA

The Greek word used is " agenetos ".

EUSTATHIUS

With one n or two?

EUSEBIUS OF NICOMEDIA

Actually, with one; but the two words are used indifferently by many theological writers.

EUSTATHIUS

There is a difference, all the same, is there not?

EUSEBIUS OF NICOMEDIA

Strictly speaking, I suppose there is.

HOSIUS

I must apologise to the Council for my bad Greek. What *is* the difference?

EUSTATHIUS

With two n's the word means " unbegotten "; with one, it means " uncreate ".

SECUNDUS

I have here a letter——

EUSTATHIUS

Secundus of Ptolemais.

SECUNDUS

—a letter from our learned brother of Nicomedia, in which he says: " Never will I call Christ *agenetos*—with one n—because that would be to assert that He is of one substance with the Father."

[At this, ATHANASIUS *and* ALEXANDER *both prick up their ears and glance towards* CONSTANTINE *and* HOSIUS. *But* HOSIUS *does not seem to have heard, and the* EMPEROR'S *face is studiously blank.* ATHANASIUS *scribbles a note, which he hands to* ALEXANDER, *who, after a glance, folds it up and passes it to* JAMES OF NISIBIS, *from whom it travels up the line of bishops until it reaches* HOSIUS.*

Perhaps Bishop Eusebius would define his use of the term?

EUSEBIUS OF NICOMEDIA

By " agenetos ", however spelt, I mean that which is underived, having no origin but in itself. This can only be predicted of the Father.

NICHOLAS

Nobody, I should imagine——

EUSTATHIUS

One moment. (*For the information of* CONSTANTINE *and the* SECRE-TARIES.) Nicholas of Myra. ·. . . Yes?

NICHOLAS

I say, nobody surely denies that the Son is *begotten* or *derived* from the Father: but that He should be thought of as a *creature*— a mere " ktismon "—is another thing altogether.

MACARIUS

Entirely different. I hope. . . . I am Macarius of Jerusalem. . . . I hope there is no attempt here to confuse the issue by the deliberate use of imprecise or ambiguous terms.

CONSTANTINE

Forgive me. But if I may intervene on behalf of the reverend Fathers from the West, as well on my own behalf as an unin-structed layman, could we not keep as far as possible to the simplest words, saying of that which is created " creature " or " made ", and of that which is procreated " begotten ", or " offspring ", or the like, so that everything may be plainly understood?

[Meantime, the note has arrived at HOSIUS, *who reads it, nods to* ALEXANDER, *and slips it into the hand of* CONSTANTINE, *as he sits*

142

down. CONSTANTINE *gives it a glance and, without any change of expression, quietly puts it away.*

VINCENT

My name is Vincent; I and my colleague Victor represent the Bishop of Rome. I should like to support His Imperial Majesty's considerate proposal. But it appears that the Presbyter Arius is himself undecided upon this point, for he says in his letter, " before the Son was *begotten or created* He did not exist ". Does Arius in fact maintain that the Son of God is a creature?

THEOGNIS

On the contrary, I understood him to maintain that the Son is fully God, though not in the same mode as the Father, but subsequent and inferior to Him.

ALEXANDER

How then can He be created? Between the being of God and the being of creatures the gulf is infinite. You see how the man contradicts himself.

EUSEBIUS OF NICOMEDIA

Would it not be well to let Arius speak for himself? Then you can question him.

EUSTATHIUS (*with a glance at* CONSTANTINE, *who nods agreement*) I am willing, if the Council is willing.

[*Cries of agreement.*

Arius, stand forward and speak.

ARIUS

I shall be only too delighted—both to defend my name from my traducers and to defend my doctrine against those who are too illiterate to understand Greek, and too indolent to study the Scriptures. Certainly, I say that the Son is " theos ", that is to say, " divine ", but not that He is " ho Theos ", that is to say, God himself. Our Latin friends who have no definite article in their woolly language may be excused for woolly thinking; but for those who speak Greek there is no excuse. For it is written: " The Lord your God is one God—there is none beside Him: He is God alone." Are we heathens and polytheists, to worship two gods, or three, or a dozen? The Father alone is eternal, underived Being, that which is—as He Himself said to Moses, " I AM THAT I AM ". And in His eternity, before all time, He begat the Son, whom St. Paul also calls, " the first-born of every creature "—not a part of Himself, since God cannot be divided, but called forth by Him out of nothing, as the Book of the Proverbs says: " The Lord possessed me in the beginning of His way; when there were no depths, I was brought forth." And this is His Logos, that is to say, His Wisdom or Word, by whose means He afterward made all things, and without whom, as St. John writes, " nothing was made that has been made ". And this Logos, being in the fullness of time joined to the body of a man, was—in the words of the Epistle to the Hebrews— " faithful to Him that made Him—so that, as it is written of Him in the Acts of the Apostles, " God hath made Jesus both Lord and Christ ".

This doctrine I received, and the Bishop of Nicomedia also from the venerable Lucian our teacher, and from the tradition of the Saints: One God and Father of all, and of Him One Son or Word, sole-begotten before all worlds. But that the Son had no beginning, or that He is equal and co-eternal with the Father, this we deny: for it is the nature of a son to be subsequent to his father, and of that which is derived to be inferior to that from which it derives. This stands to reason, and for this cause the Word when He was made flesh said plainly: " My Father is greater than I."

That is the truth of Scripture, which every sincere mind must acknowledge. As for Alexander, he too at one time believed and taught the same. But he has changed his tune—I do not know why, unless to curry favour with an influential party in Egypt, and so obtain the bishopric to which I had a better title. So knowing that he has injured me, he hates and persecutes me, and in hope to discredit me has embraced the abominable heresy of the Sabellians, which denies altogether the distinct personality not only of the Son, but of Father and Spirit too, treating all these as mere abstractions or aspects of an undifferentiated Godhead. For this I rebuked him, in that sermon of which he complains. But his whole pursuit of me is sheer jealous spite, unless it is senility and softening of the brain, which is the most charitable explanation I can suggest. But let him deny if he can that when he thought honestly he thought and taught as I do. (*He remains standing.*)

144

ALEXANDER (*shaking with rage and agitation*)

It is false! I deny it absolutely. This man—a priest in my own diocese—bringing these shameful accusations! Never, never did I envy him, or change my opinions to secure preferment, or favour the Sabellian heresy. (ATHANASIUS *passes him a paper.*) Nor did I ever teach his pernicious doctrine. What I said—I call Heaven to witness—I said that the Father—the Son is of the Father—— (*He tries to read the note* ATHANASIUS *has handed to him, but is too much overcome.*) That I should be called senile and corrupt—before the Emperor and the whole Church!—— (*He bursts into tears and sits down.*) Tell them, tell them, Athanasius.

ATHANASIUS (*rising with paper in hand*)

Have I your permission, reverend Fathers, to read to you what my venerable Father-in-God would have said, had not this cruel personal attack prostrated him?

EUSTATHIUS

We will hear the Deacon Athanasius.

ATHANASIUS

First, then, ignoring the personal abuse which our opponent drags in to bolster up the weakness of his cause, the Bishop would have me say this. That the Son derives from the Father is true, for the Father is Being Itself, the fount and substance of all being, whether in Heaven or earth. This indeed Alexander has always believed and taught. But the Son is not subsequent to the Father, for His begetting is from eternity, where time is not, and where there is no time there is neither before nor after. This, Arius himself confusedly admits, when he says " before all times, before all ages "—though he had better have said " without time ", since where time is excluded the word " before " has no meaning. And further, when Arius says " it is of the nature of a son to be subsequent to his father ", Alexander would reply: " God is not a man with limbs and members, to change and grow old like a man, or beget after the fashion of men. God is spirit, and that which derives from Him is spirit also, begotten of him as the ray is begotten of the light. The ray derives from the light, not subsequently, but simultaneously; and as there is no ray without light, so there is no light without the ray. Neither is the ray inferior to the light, for it *is* light—

light out of light, from the very substance and being of light, as the Son is God out of God, from the very substance and Being of God; therefore the blessed Apostle, in his Epistle to the Hebrews, calls Him: " the brightness of the Father's glory and the express image of His person, upholding all things by the word of His power." And the Apostle John, in the beginning of his Gospel which lies here open before you, declares very well both the distinct Person of the Son and His equal Godhead with the Father, saying: " In the beginning was the Word, and the Word was *with* God, and the Word *was* God."

ARIUS

Why, then, does the Apostle call Him " the first-born of every creature "?

ATHANASIUS

Because so He is. For when He became Man, He made Himself as one of the creatures; and therefore He said of himself when He was in the body, " My Father is greater than I ", because He had assumed our nature, being made a little lower than the angels. As it is written, " The first man was of the earth, earthy: the second Man is the Lord from Heaven ". Yet He Himself created the nature that He put on; and this was ordained by Him from eternity when time was not, so that He that is second on earth is first in Heaven. Who also went up thither, the first-born from the dead of all that He had created. Him likewise did John behold in his Apocalypse, in form like unto the Son of Man, and saying, " I am Alpha and Omega, the beginning and the ending, saith the Lord, which is and which was and which is to come, the Almighty ".

ARIUS

Spoken like a giant, little mannikin. You are so learned in the Scripture you know more about it than Christ Himself, who said to the rich young ruler: " Why callest thou me good? There is none good but one, that is, God."

ATHANASIUS

So he did—and the fool stood gaping. But what if he had answered, like Peter: " Thou art the Christ, the Son of the living God "?

He would have earned a blessing—and perhaps have been commended for knowing better than to confuse the Son with the Father.

ATHANASIUS

Was Thomas, then, rebuked when, looking upon the wounds of the Redeemer, he cried: " My Lord and my God! "? Rebuked he was, not for belief, but because he was so slow in believing. . . . And do not forget to remind your Latin friends, with your customary politeness, that he said, not " theos " but " ho theos mou "—" the Lord of me and the God of me"—with the definite article, Arius.

[*Here* CONSTANTINE *and the* WESTERN BISHOPS *burst out laughing, at which* ARIUS *looks so disconcerted that everybody joins in.*

CONSTANTINE

You had him there, Athanasius.

HOSIUS

Between the joints of the harness.

CONSTANTINE

But this bow was not drawn at a venture.

[*Everybody is greatly impressed by the* EMPEROR'S *ready wit and familiarity with the Scriptures.*

ATHANASIUS

Well, Arius, what do you say?

ARIUS (*rallying as best he can*)

I say that, after the Resurrection, the image of the Father's Person being clearly stamped upon the glorified Body——

ATHANASIUS

Indeed? Was it the likeness of the *Father* that was seen in the print of the nails? And it was *before* the Resurrection that Our Lord said to Philip: " He that hath seen Me hath seen the Father."

147

That, too, is said of the image—as a man may be recognised by his reflection in a glass.

ATHANASIUS

It seems you would deny the Son any real existence at all. . . . And when He said to His disciples, " I and My Father are one "?

ARIUS

He meant that they were like-minded, in that He did the will of the Father. For in Him the image was uniquely perfect, not being distorted by a fallible human soul.

[ATHANASIUS *is so astonished that he can hardly believe his ears. But he leaps on this indiscretion like a cat on a rat.*

ATHANASIUS

You say that Christ had no human soul?

ARIUS

In Christ, the Logos took the place of the human soul.

ATHANASIUS

Then was He not true man, for man's nature consists in a fleshly body and a rational soul. There are heretics who deny Christ's Godhead and others who deny His Manhood—it was left for Arius to deny both at once. . . . Tell me, how did this compound of half-man and demi-god do the will of the Father? Freely, or of necessity?

ARIUS (*hesitating—he sees the trap but cannot avoid it*)
Freely.

ATHANASIUS

That which is created free to stand is created free to fall. Was the Son, then, made fallible by nature, needing God's grace to keep Him from sin? If so, the second Adam is no more than the first, Christ is but man—or at most an angel—and to worship Him is idolatry.

ARIUS (*sullenly*)

I did not say that.

I am glad to hear it. But if He was created infallible, then He was not free, but did the Father's will of necessity, as the brutes do, and brute matter.

ARIUS

I say that He was made of like will with the Father, and therefore He cannot err.

ATHANASIUS

You mean that His nature is its own necessity?

ARIUS

Yes.

ATHANASIUS

Then He is God, for only God is His own necessity. . . . Beloved Fathers, in whom will you believe? In the Christ of Arius, who is neither true Man to bear our sorrows nor true God to forgive us our sins? Or in Him who, being in the form of God, clung not to His equality with God, but was made in the likeness of man and became obedient unto death for our sakes? Reasoning is but words—God's act is the living truth. I call upon the martyrs to say for whom they suffered.

AMPHION

For Christ our God.

PAUL

For Christ our God.

PAPHNUTIUS

For Christ who is over all, God blessed for ever.

ATHANASIUS

So speaks Paul the Apostle. So speak those who shed their blood for Christ. But what says Arius? Would you, Paphnutius, comfort your heart with this song of his? Would you, James of Nisibis, send it echoing across the wilderness? Or you, Spiridion, sing it when you pasture your flocks by clear waters?

"Arius of Alexandria, I'm the talk of all the town,
  Friend of saints, elect of Heaven, filled with learning and
                                                    renown;
  If you want the Logos-doctrine, I can serve it hot and hot:
  God begat Him and before He was begotten, He was not."

  [*The* BISHOPS *put their fingers in their ears.*

149

BISHOPS (*except the* ARIANS)

Blasphemous! Horrible! Away with it!

ATHANASIUS

There are several more verses. Shall I go on?

BISHOPS (*as before*)

No! No!

ATHANASIUS

Shall I tear it up?

BISHOPS (*as before*)

Tear it! tear it—and the letter too!

[ATHANASIUS *tears the song. The Council is in a tumult.* EUSEBIUS OF NICOMEDIA, *looking very white, gets up, dropping* ARIUS's *letter, which is immediately seized upon and torn to shreds.* EUSEBIUS *goes to* ARIUS *and pulls him over to where the other* ARIANS *are sitting.*

ATHANASIUS *goes back to* ALEXANDER, *who appears to congratulate him.*

EUSEBIUS OF NICOMEDIA

It's no good, Arius. We must pull what we can out of the wreck.

[*When the commotion has subsided,* EUSEBIUS OF CAESAREA *is found to be on his feet and speaking.*

EUSEBIUS OF CAESAREA

. . . consequently I suggest that I should lay before the Council the baptismal symbol used in my own diocese of Caesarea, to serve as a basis for discussion. (*He remains standing throughout the ensuing debate.*)

EUSTATHIUS

Let us take it clause by clause.

EUSEBIUS OF CAESAREA

"We believe in One God, the Father Almighty, Maker of all things visible and invisible." (*He pauses, and as nobody offers any objection, resumes.*) "And in One Lord Jesus Christ, the Word of God——"

JOHN

I suggest the substitution of "Son" for "Word" in that clause, to avoid at once any suggestion of the impersonal or the abstract.

NICHOLAS

I second that. "Son" will suit better with the word "begotten" which has to follow.

EUSEBIUS OF CAESAREA

"Only-begotten Son" comes in later.

HOSIUS

Let us get it quite clear from the start. I propose "the Son of God, sole-begotten of the Father".

[*The* BISHOPS *assent.*

EUSEBIUS OF CAESAREA

Very well.

[*The* SECRETARIES *write down the amendment.*

Next comes: "God out of God, Light out of Light, Life out of Life, Son only-begotten. . . ." We've got that in already.

PAPHNUTIUS

In view of the debate we have heard, I should like to see "True God out of True God" inserted after "Light out of Light".

EUSEBIUS OF CAESAREA

In addition to "Life out of Life"?

VICTOR

That is virtually included in "begotten"—all life begets life.

PAUL

Do we really need "Light out of Light"?

EUSTATHIUS

I think that's important; it defines the mode of begetting.

PAUL

True.

EUSTATHIUS

Any objection to "True God out of True God"?

EUSEBIUS OF NICOMEDIA

None. We have always asserted Christ's true divinity.

[*The amendment is carried and noted as before.*

EUSEBIUS OF CAESAREA

Omitting, then, "Son only-begotten"

[*All signify agreement.*

we go straight on. "First-born of every creature before all ages."

SEVERAL VOICES (*very loudly*)

No.

SECUNDUS

Yes.

EUSEBIUS OF NICOMEDIA (*to* SECUNDUS)

Be quiet. It doesn't matter what they *leave out*.

EUSEBIUS OF CAESAREA

The phrase is Scriptural.

NICHOLAS

We have seen that it is open to misconstruction.

JOHN

I am not sure that it doesn't really mean "born prior to all creatures".

HOSIUS

It seems to be ambiguous.

EUSTATHIUS

I agree. Better leave it out.

[*All signify agreement. Amendment noted.*

Next clause?

EUSEBIUS OF CAESAREA

"Begotten from the Father."

EUSTATHIUS

We've had that: no need to repeat it.

152

SPIRIDION

That's where we want to put in, "begotten, not made".

[*Everybody is electrified.*

NICHOLAS

Well done, Spiridion!

EUSTATHIUS

Well spoken, shepherd of Cyprus!

HOSIUS

Yes. We want no more trouble with the number of n's in "genetos".

[*Laughter and applause. The amendment is carried by acclamation.*

ARIUS (*to* EUSEBIUS OF NICOMEDIA)

Won't you protest?

EUSEBIUS OF NICOMEDIA

No, no, what's the good? It would only make matters worse.

EUSEBIUS OF CAESAREA

"Begotten, not made, by whom also all things were made. Who for our salvation——"

EUSTATHIUS

One moment. Are we now sufficiently definite? We have said "True God out of True God"—is there anything more to add about the unity of the Father and the Son?

AMPHION

I suggest we might add "Image of the Father's Person".

[*There is a small buzz of private discussion.*

EUSEBIUS OF NICOMEDIA (*to the* ARIANS)

Let it go. Man also is made in the image of God.

JOHN

Perhaps, "in all things like unto the Father" would be better.

[*More discussion.*

ARIUS (*to* EUSEBIUS OF NICOMEDIA *and other* ARIANS)

That is the same as "in the image", and gets them no further.

How about "being the eternal power of the Father"?

[*Discussion as before.*

ARIUS (*as before*)

Power? Why, the caterpillar and the locust are in Scripture called "power", and it is said also of the people of God.

ALEXANDER

Can we not say, "being from eternity One with the Father"—for He says, "I and My Father are One".

THEOGNIS (*to* ARIANS)

He prayed also that His disciples might be "one" with Him, as He and His Father were one.

SECUNDUS

And eternally; for it is written: "Who shall separate us?"

EUSTATHIUS

Any objections?

EUSEBIUS OF NICOMEDIA (*aloud*)

How can anybody object to so scriptural and inoffensive an expression?

ALEXANDER

You see, brethren—these men will agree to anything, so long as they can interpret it in their own way. (*To* ARIANS) You need not look so self-righteous—I can see you nodding and winking to one another, blind and senile as I may be.

CONSTANTINE

Will you give me leave to speak?

EUSTATHIUS

But of course, sir. Pray do.

CONSTANTINE

There was a phrase mentioned earlier in the proceedings which struck me very forcibly. It was, if I remember it rightly, "of one substance with the Father".

154

Oh lord!

HOSIUS

Why, yes, sir—"consubstantial"—quite a familiar term in the West. The Greek, I believe, is "homosoious". (*He pronounces it to rhyme with "joyous".*)

CONSTANTINE (*deprecatingly*)

"Homo-ousios", I think.

HOSIUS

I told you my Greek was bad. Your Majesty is of course quite right.

[*The word has taken everybody rather aback—but since it is the Emperor's suggestion nobody likes to speak first. Murmurs.*

CONSTANTINE (*insinuatingly*)

It seems to me a very definite and unambiguous sort of word.

ARIUS (*to* ARIANS)

And I took that man for a simpleton!

CONSTANTINE

As the Apostle says, I speak as a fool—there may be objections to it.

EUSEBIUS OF NICOMEDIA (*to* ARIANS)

They've put him up to it. (*Aloud*) There is every objection to it.

[*Glances are exchanged. At last the* ARIANS *are showing fight.*

EUSEBIUS OF CAESAREA (*hesitatingly*)

It is not scriptural.

ARIUS (*with satisfaction*)

Ah!

POTAMON

I must say with all due deference, I don't care much about using a word that isn't in the Scriptures.

VOICE (*loudly off*)

It is also heretical.

155

Who is that, please?

Maris of Chalcedon. The word was condemned at Antioch.

In a totally different connection.

What was that?

In the controversy with Paul of Samosata; it was thought then to have a Sabellian flavour, as tending to confound the Persons of the Godhead.

But the danger now is the other way round.

The word "consubstantial" has been used for years in Rome and throughout the West. There has never been any trouble about it.

The authority of the Bishop of Rome is very great.

Western theology is beneath contempt and always has been.

Really!

We can always safeguard our use of the phrase by other expressions.

But it remains unscriptural.

Do you think you know better than the Holy Ghost? Which will you have? The Word of God or the word of Constantine?

[*Everybody is shocked, except* CONSTANTINE.

CONSTANTINE (*mildly*)

Nobody, I hope, would hesitate. But I did not invent the word. . . .
What does Athanasius say?

ATHANASIUS

Surely it is not a question of substituting our words for those of the
Holy Spirit, but only of defining with exactness our understanding
of what the Spirit says in symbols and mysteries. And Our Lord
Himself set us the example when He interpreted to His disciples
the parables which He had taught them.

JAMES

Do not we all do as He did? When I preach to my simple desert
folk, I tell them a story, or read them a psalm, and then I say,
"this is how we must understand it".

SEVERAL VOICES

Quite right.

ATHANASIUS

I should—that is, my Bishop would—greatly prefer a scriptural
word. But our urgent need just now is of a word that nobody can
possibly misinterpret—not even Arius.

SECUNDUS

I will never accept "homoöusios".

[*Assenting and dissenting cries.*

EUSTATHIUS

Will those Bishops who repudiate the expression "homoöusios"
or "consubstantial" please stand up.

[EUSEBIUS OF NICOMEDIA, THEOGNIS, SECUNDUS, THEONAS, *with
others off-stage, stand.* EUSEBIUS OF CAESAREA *seems to hesitate and
then abruptly sits down.* SECRETARIES *count.*

SECRETARY-DEACON

Seventeen.

EUSTATHIUS

Seventeen out of three hundred and eighteen. The phrase is
accepted.

[*Hum of approbation.*

157

HOSIUS

It might be well, in the earlier clause, to define "begotten" in that sense.

[*Agreement.*

EUSTATHIUS

Continue, Eusebius.

EUSEBIUS OF CAESAREA (*rising, in a colourless voice*)

"Begotten, not made, being consubstantial with the Father, by Whom also all things were made."

[ATHANASIUS *has passed a note to* ALEXANDER.

ALEXANDER

Let us add, "both things in Heaven and things in earth". Otherwise, somebody will point out that the Angels too are called "the sons of God". But the Only-Begotten made the Angels.

[*Agreement. Another note from* ATHANASIUS *to* ALEXANDER.

EUSEBIUS OF CAESAREA

"Who for our salvation was made flesh———"

ALEXANDER

"*Came down* and was made flesh"—or this time we shall be told that before He was born on earth He was not.

[*Agreement.*

EUSEBIUS OF CAESAREA

"Came down and was made flesh, and lived among men and suffered."

ALEXANDER

May we not add "lived among men *as man*". Not a half-man, or an imitation man, as we heard suggested just now.

[*Agreement as before.*

EUSEBIUS OF CAESAREA

Do you wish to amend the final clauses?

EUSTATHIUS

I think every point is now covered. I will read the draft as amended.

[Secretary hands it to him.

"We believe in One God, the Father Almighty, Maker of all things visible and invisible. And in One Lord Jesus Christ, the Son of God, sole-begotten of the Father's substance, God out of God, Light out of Light, True God out of True God, begotten not made, consubstantial with the Father. By Whom also all things were made, both things in Heaven and things in earth. Who for us men and our salvation came down and was made flesh, lived among men as man, suffered, and rose again the third day, ascended into Heaven, and cometh to judge the quick and the dead.

And we believe in the Holy Ghost."

Take the draft down the room for the signatures of those who accept it.

[At this, EUSEBIUS OF NICOMEDIA *rises, and begins to retreat across the room in the direction of his original seat.*

SECUNDUS

You will not sign it, Eusebius!

EUSEBIUS OF NICOMEDIA

What can I do? The Church has spoken.

ARIUS

The Emperor has spoken.

THEOGNIS

We can always say that we understood "homoöusios" in the sense "homoiousios".

EUSEBIUS OF NICOMEDIA

True—between "of *one* substance" and "of *like* substance" there is the difference only of an iota.

[Meanwhile, the DEACON-SECRETARY *has taken the paper to* HOSIUS, *and is proceeding down that side of the room.* EUSEBIUS OF NICOMEDIA *catches him on his way, signs hurriedly, and goes to his old seat.* TOGI, *however, has taken his copy down off-stage to the other side of the room, and is working up in the opposite direction, so that it will come last to the* ARIAN *group.*

SECUNDUS

I will never sign.

159

And now, I suppose we proceed to the anathemas. (*He writes.*)

THEOGNIS

You may be thankful now, Arius, that you missed that bishopric. Your signature will not be demanded.

ARIUS

I should not care if it was. I would not turn traitor, Theognis, as I see you mean to do. (*He beckons* ATHANASIUS, *who crosses to him.*) Do you think I care for the Emperor? Alexander and this fellow were the prompters to him, but he will soon forget his part. Put not your trust in princes, mannikin. They use you for their political ends, and when it suits them they turn away and leave you to face the music.

ATHANASIUS

The Faith shall be maintained, Arius, were it by Athanasius against the world.

EUSTATHIUS (*rising and reading what he has written*)

"And those who say, 'Once He was not', or 'Before His begetting He was not', or 'He came into existence out of nothing'; and those who pretend that the Son of God is 'of other substance', or 'created', or 'mutable', or 'alterable', them the Catholic Church anathematizes, and let them be anathema."

[*Agreement signified.*

CONSTANTINE

While we are waiting, may I take this opportunity of inviting you all——

[TOGI'S *copy of the creed has now reached the* ARIANS. THEOGNIS *signs, but not* SECUNDUS *or* THEONAS.

——everybody, that is, who is not anathematized or banished—to dine with Us in the Palace, on the first day after the conclusion of the Council.

EUSTATHIUS

Your Majesty is most gracious.

[TOGI *has now collected the signatures of* NICASIAS *and* EUSTATHIUS: *and the* DEACON-SECRETARY *has come up and joined him.*

How many dissentients?

Two only have refused to sign: Secundus of Ptolemais and Theonas of Marmarica.

EUSTATHIUS

Then it is my duty to pronounce on them, as also on the Presbyter Arius, the Church's sentence of anathema, excommunication and deprivation.

ARIUS (*sarcastically*)

"And his bishopric let another take."

CONSTANTINE

With that we have nothing to do, but their banishment is Our responsibility. See to it, Philumenos.

[PHILUMENOS, *an officer of the Household, steps forward and shepherds the delinquents off by the way the brazier came in.*

Does this end the day's session?

EUSTATHIUS

If it please Your Majesty. (*Announcing*) The Council is dissolved until tomorrow.

ALL (*rising*)

Glory be to the Father, and to the Son, and to the Holy Ghost, as it was in the beginning, is now, and ever shall be, world without end. Amen.

SCENE 6

A.D. 325—*Nicaea: a part of the Imperial garden, on a July evening.*

[*Enter* HELENA *and* MATIBENA, *walking.*

HELENA (*laying her hand on* MATIBENA's *arm*)

Matibena, I am frightened.

MATIBENA

I have been afraid for a long time, my lady.

HELENA

I have been afraid from the beginning. But now I am frightened.

MATIBENA

What of?

HELENA

The goddess Aphrodite. (*She sits down by the door.*)

MATIBENA (*startled*)

The goddess? What heathen talk's that?

HELENA

The gods of Olympus are not fables. They are fallen angels, full of malice and glitter and power. And cruel, cruel, Matibena.

MATIBENA (*defensively*)

A lot of nasty, naked statues, which I wouldn't dignify by looking at 'em.

HELENA

Love deprived of its worship turns to hatred.

MATIBENA

Common human sinfulness, that's what it is, never mind angels and goddesses. Couldn't you speak to her?

HELENA

She resents me too much already. That's why I try to live privately and keep out of the public eye as much as possible. One mustn't seem to compete, or to interfere. . . . I've tried speaking to *him*—but it's not the kind of thing he understands.

MATIBENA

I don't know what she has to complain of. It's not as though he ran after other women.

HELENA

It might be easier for her, poor child, if he did. She would know better than how to hurt him. He loves in the pious old Roman fashion—" my wife, my family, my empire, my religion "—institutions rather than people. Such men are not readily vulnerable.

MATIBENA (*abandoning this psychological problem*)
What's bothering me is all this plotting going on.

HELENA
Ah! . . . you think there's something?

MATIBENA
I know there is, my lady, and it scares me out of my life. It's all that Bassiana Marcia—horrid sly creature. She ought to have been bundled out neck and crop a long time ago.

HELENA
Yes.

MATIBENA
I used to think there was something between her and Licinius—but his teeth have been drawn, thank goodness. "That'll put a stop to your games, my girl," I said to myself. But now she's going about licking her lips like a cat in the pantry. . . . I don't know why people want to be emperors—nothing but wars and worries, and expecting to be poisoned every time you sit down to a meal. It'd take my appetite away.

HELENA (*seriously*)
I had thought of that. But somehow I don't think it's likely. When you hate somebody you once loved, you don't want to kill him. You want to see him suffer—even if it makes you suffer yourself.

MATIBENA
What do you know about such nasty wicked feelings? You've never wanted to hurt anybody.
[*Enter* FAUSTA.

HELENA
Don't be too sure of that, Matibena. . . . Were you looking for me, my dear?

FAUSTA
When's Crispus coming home?

HELENA (*surprised*)
Crispus? I don't know. When he can be spared from his military duties on the frontier. There's a little trouble, you know, on the Danube.

FAUSTA

Tiresome barbarians! . . . I suppose he'll manage to get back
next year for the Vicennalia celebrations.

HELENA

Oh, dear, yes—I should hope so. Do you particularly want to
see him?

FAUSTA

Crispus is the only person in this household who's reasonably
polite to one. Horses and soldiers and dogs come first, of course,
but (*venomously*) at least he isn't actively rude.

HELENA

Has something upset you, my dear?

FAUSTA

Oh no, I'm used to it. (*Breaking out*) Really, Constantine's
temper gets worse and worse. One of these days he'll murder
somebody, if he's not careful.

HELENA

He is sometimes a little hasty. But it's soon over. You mustn't
pay any attention.

FAUSTA

I merely suggested to him that he might stay and give me a little
of his attention, instead of galloping off tonight to Chrysopolis
to review troops at crack of dawn, and he went right up in
smoke. (*She imitates* CONSTANTINE *rather wickedly*) " Don't act
like a courtesan. Kindly remember that you are Augusta and
My Wife "—I thought he was going to bite me.

MATIBENA

You didn't ought to nag at him, my lady, if you'll excuse me.
Gentlemen with their minds full of armies and politics can't be
always loving and paying compliments—not old married
gentlemen, anyhow.

FAUSTA

Mamma!

164

HELENA

Matibena, you are forgetting yourself. You had better go.

[MATIBENA *goes.*

FAUSTA

She's a vulgar old woman, and you encourage her to insult me.

HELENA

No, dear. But she's getting on for eighty, and I don't like to be harsh with her. She nursed me from a baby, and we all seem like children to her. And you know, there's a good deal in what she says.

FAUSTA

I'm unhappy.

HELENA (*getting up and going to her*)

Yes, I know you are. Couldn't you tell me about it?

FAUSTA

You'd only take Constantine's side.

HELENA (*smiling*)

Not necessarily, I assure you.

FAUSTA

And you'd talk about Christ. I don't want to hear about Christ. People shouldn't let themselves be crucified. They should stand up for themselves and fight back.

[*Enter* BASSIANA MARCIA.

Oh, Marcia, I don't really want my cloak.

MARCIA

The evening air is treacherous, my lady.

FAUSTA

I am stifled with heat. I think there is a storm coming up.

[HELENA *turns to go.*

Good night, Mamma.

Good night.

[*Exit* HELENA.

MARCIA

When, madam?

FAUSTA

At the Vicennalia, almost certainly.

MARCIA

That will do very well.

FAUSTA

Give me my cloak. I am shivering. I must have a touch of fever.
Or perhaps it is only the storm.

MARCIA

Come to bed.

[*Exeunt.*

SCENE 7

July, 325—*Nicaea: a banqueting-hall in the Palace.* ($\frac{1}{2}$ *set A.*)

[CONSTANTINE, *attended, receives the* BISHOPS *who are dining with
him. Each* BISHOP, *as he is brought forward, kisses his hand.*

CONSTANTINE

A most hearty welcome to all my friends! . . . No need to
announce them—by this time I know and love them all. . . .
Welcome, dear Eustathius, Our right hand in Our counsels,
now Our right hand at the feast. . . . Welcome, Theognis of
Nicaea—you are Our fellow-host in this, your see of Nicaea. . . .
Welcome, James of Nisibis—for once forgo the diet of the
anchorites and condescend to our worldly fare. . . . Welcome,
good Nicholas of Myra, you, I know, are one that likes to make
merry. . . .

[PAPHNUTIUS *comes limping forward.* CONSTANTINE *comes down
from the steps to meet him.*

No, no, Paphnutius—who are We that Christ's
martyrs should kneel to Us? (*He kisses his blinded eye.*) Give me
your blessing, most dear and honoured Father in God.

God bless you, my dear son, and bring you quickly out of the heathen wilderness into the fold of His baptism.

CONSTANTINE

Amen, Paphnutius. I hope it may be soon. . . . I know that it grieves you all that I cannot, as yet, make myself wholly Christ's. But, as you are the Bishops of those within the Church, I am Bishop of those without, who have no shepherd and no High Priest but me. For a little time longer I must needs be all things to all men. But I will tell you one thing. Next year I celebrate my Vicennalia in Rome. Twenty years shall I have worn the purple, and during that time God has wrought much for His Church by my hand. The glory is His alone. And in token of gratitude to Him We mean to transfer Our Imperial seat to Byzantium. There We shall raise up a new Rome, built afresh from the foundations, that shall never have known a heathen temple or acknowledged any God but Christ. And in time We shall wean all Our people from their false worship, and there shall be but one throne and one altar, one City and one Church, and Christ the Ruler of all.

BISHOPS

Amen. God save the Emperor.

[*The reception continues as the curtains close.*

SCENE 8

A.D. 326—*Rome: an anteroom in the Palace. Night.* ($\frac{1}{2}$ *set B.*)

BASSIANA MARCIA (*entering through a curtain and turning to speak to somebody within*)

Play your part well. (*She looks towards the door and beckons. Enter a* SLAVE GIRL.) Go and tell the Lord Crispus that the Lady Fausta is ready to receive him. And send Crito to me.

[*Exit* SLAVE.

Dilly-dilly-dilly, come and be killed. First the sprat and then the big herring. Rome is ready for you, Constantine—you shall have a merry Vicennalia, believe me. The garlands are hung out, the altars are decked, the priest awaits the sacrifice, and the victim is here. Hold down his head, Constantine, Pontifex Maximus; he is an offering to the gods below. (*She takes wine from a table and sprinkles it on the floor.*) A libation to Proserpine! (*She stoops to the ground and whispers*) Wake up your Furies, Queen of Hell. Do you hear me, ancient mothers? Are your snakes stirring? Avenge my brother, avenge Maximian, avenge Maxentius, avenge the gods! Avenge the soul I am sending you! (*She listens, and stands upright as* SLAVE *enters, with* CRISPUS.)

CRISPUS

Augusta wishes to see me?

MARCIA

Yes, lord. . . . You are leaving Rome tonight?

CRISPUS

At daybreak. I am to meet the Emperor at Pola.

MARCIA

She has been anxious to see you before you went, to send some message, I think, to His Majesty. But do not be surprised if you find her a little drowsy and fanciful. She has been feverish all day, and the physician has given her a sleeping-draught.

CRISPUS

I am sorry.

MARCIA

It is nothing. The air of Rome is full of malarial agues, and she is subject to them. Go in, my lord. (*She holds back the curtain for him to enter, and we see* FAUSTA *lying on a couch, with a small lamp beside her.*) Is Crito here?

SLAVE

Yes.

[*Enter* CRITO, *a slave.* MARCIA *speaks to him apart.*

MARCIA

You know the house of the Senator Crassus?

CRITO

Yes, lady.

MARCIA

The Lord Crispus leaves Rome at daybreak. When he is gone, and not before, deliver this packet to Crassus, into his own hand, privately. He will reward you for your service.

CRITO

Yes, lady.

[*He takes the packet and goes.*

MARCIA

Listen! What's that?

[*From behind the curtain comes a sound of incoherent speech and hysterical sobbing, ending with a series of loud screams.* CRISPUS *emerges, looking rather alarmed.*

CRISPUS

Marcia!

MARCIA

What's the matter?

CRISPUS

She is delirious, I'm afraid.

MARCIA (*to the* SLAVE)

Go to your mistress.

[SLAVE *goes in.*

CRISPUS

She was rambling and muttering when I went in. When I spoke to her, it seemed to make her worse. She didn't know me. She mistook me for an assassin, I think. (*He laughs a little awkwardly.*) A sort of nightmare, or something.

MARCIA

Poor dear! It's the drug she has taken. Syrup of poppies often affects people that way at first—but they sleep soundly afterwards. . . . So she couldn't give you the message?

[CRISPUS *shakes his head.*

Don't worry—I think the whole thing was all just a feverish fancy. . . . It's nothing serious. I wouldn't bother Augustus about it.

[*The sounds from within have ceased. She lifts the curtain.*

There! you see she is sleeping peacefully now. The drug is working well.

That's good. Poor Augusta!—give her my love when she wakes. No, of course I shan't say anything to my father. It's only a touch of fever. . . . Well, I must be going. Good night, Marcia.

MARCIA

Good night, my lord.

[*Exit* CRISPUS.

. . . Now—a swift gig and the best post-horses to take me to Pola, and with luck I'll be there before you—Prince Hippolytus.

SCENE 9

Rome—next morning. A room in the Palace.

[*Enter* TOGI, *in a hurry, with a ship's manifest. He sits down at the table and begins checking items.*

TOGI

Five hundred barrels of wine . . . a thousand bushels of wheat . . .

MATIBENA (*calling off*)

Togi! Togi!

TOGI

Blast the woman! . . . Twelve bales of cloth, dyed Tyrian purple— I'm sure we ordered fifteen. . . .

MATIBENA

Togi! Togi! (*Entering breathless.*) Oh, *there* you are! I've been hunting for you all over the Palace.

TOGI (*shortly*)

I was down at the docks. . . . Six cases spice, four ditto best pepper . . .

MATIBENA

Togi, for God's sake——

TOGI

What *is* the matter now? I'm busy. I've got all these Festival accounts to see to. . . . What on earth has become of those barrels of British oysters . . . ?

Leave that rubbish and look at this.

TOGI

What? (*Taking paper from her.*) Where did you get this?

MATIBENA

From that Marcia's slave-boy, Crito. . . . I gave him a drink, and slipped something into it that will keep him snoring till noon.

TOGI (*horrified*)

Augusta's own seal! . . . Matibena, you'll get into trouble for this.

MATIBENA

Who's it addressed to?

TOGI

The Senator Crassus. . . . (*An uncomfortable thought strikes him.*) Crassus . . . He's of the old Roman party—a heathen and known to be disaffected. Why should Augusta be writing to Crassus?

MATIBENA

Open it and see.

TOGI

I daren't do that, Matibena.

MATIBENA

I dare. (*She snatches it back and breaks the seal.*) There! Quick! Don't waste time! (*Shaking him violently.*) Oh! if only I knew how to read!

[TOGI *slowly and doubtfully opens the letter and stares transfixed.*

TOGI

Good God!

MATIBENA

What is it? Speak, you booby—don't sit gaping at it.

TOGI (*reads*)

"Fausta to Crassus: I have today dispatched the message that shall make a Hippolytus of Crispus. Send the enclosed to

Licinius. On the first day of the Vicennalia, strike. But spare the life of Constantine—I loved him once".... The Lord Christ be merciful to us!

MATIBENA

I knew it, I knew it. I knew they were plotting something.

TOGI

Well—we're warned. Our friend Crassus will get a surprise on the first day of the Festival. Licinius is raising an army, I suppose—what a hope! But that Augusta should be involved——

MATIBENA

What about Crispus? What's a Hippolytus?

TOGI

One of their heathen fables, I expect.

MATIBENA (*urgently*)

Whatever the message is, it's gone.

TOGI

So it has.

MATIBENA

Bassiana Marcia left the city at midnight—secretly, with swift horses. I saw her—though she didn't see me.... What dreadful kind of thing can a Hippolytus be?

TOGI

I don't know. I only know the Bible.

MATIBENA (*wringing her hands*)

Oh, I wish we were all pagans and going to Hell, if only we could find out.... Wait—look—there's my mistress. She may know. She knows lots of things. Give me the letters. (*She seizes them and rushes out.*)

TOGI (*fidgeting distractedly with the papers on the table*)

Oysters and Tyrian purple—I was worrying my head about oysters!... Oh, Constantine, my dear master, this will hit you hard....

[*Enter* HELENA *and* MATIBENA.

172

Togi—take these papers and ride instantly with them to Constantine. You are riding for the life of Crispus—and you are starting nine hours late.

CENTER TOGI

For the life of Crispus?

CENTER HELENA

Hippolytus, son of Theseus, King of Troezene, was accused by his stepmother Phaedra of an incestuous assault upon her. So Theseus in his rage, not waiting to hear the truth, sent Hippolytus to his death. . . . You know Constantine's temper. Make haste. . . . Have you got money?

CENTER TOGI (*taking a bag from the table*)

Plenty. (*He plunges out.*)

CENTER HELENA (*falling back into* MATIBENA'S *arms*)

God send he is in time.

[*They wait, clinging together. Presently the hoofbeats of* TOGI'S *horse are heard. They die away into the distance.*]

SCENE 10

A.D. 326—*Constantine's Lodging in Pola. Evening, with a red sunset.*
(½ *set A.*)

[CONSTANTINE; *and* CRISPUS *guarded by two* SOLDIERS.

CENTER CONSTANTINE (*reading from a slip of paper*)

"My messenger will tell you what shame will not let me write. Avenge your honour." . . . In the face of that, do you still maintain your innocence?

CENTER CRISPUS (*hotly*)

Of course I am innocent. How can you even imagine such beastliness?

CENTER CONSTANTINE

My virtuous son—who has no leman of his own but dedicates his spoils to Augusta. . . . Will you deny that two nights since, you forced yourself into your stepmother's bedroom——?

CRISPUS

I did nothing of the sort. She sent for me.

CONSTANTINE

Beast and liar! Would you fasten the filth on *her*? . . . Did you not assault her and did she not cry out for help? Were you not caught there, with your dress disordered——?

CRISPUS

She was sick and delirious and took me for an assassin.

CONSTANTINE

Sick? And you said nothing of it?

CRISPUS

It was only a touch of the fever. Father, in God's name——

CONSTANTINE

Father! Yes, I am your father, and you have dishonoured your father's bed.

CRISPUS

As Christ lives, I have not. This is a trick—a plot. But I have witnesses.

CONSTANTINE

What witnesses?

CRISPUS

My mother's slave, and Bassiana Marcia.

CONSTANTINE

Bassiana Marcia? It is she who accuses you.

[BASSIANA MARCIA *steps out from behind a curtain.*

MARCIA

You shall not make me a partner in your crime, Lord Crispus. I say you are guilty.

CRISPUS

Perjurer, speak the truth.

174

I have, and call the gods to witness.

Then I am lost.

[CONSTANTINE *signs to the* SOLDIERS, *who close in upon* CRISPUS.

Father! For Christ's sake, for your own soul's sake——

CONSTANTINE

Blasphemer!

CRISPUS

Listen! Do not murder me. . . . I am your son—how could I dream of injuring you? I am a Christian—how could I even imagine such a horror as this they accuse me of? Will you believe this heathen woman, your enemy and sister to your enemy——?

CONSTANTINE

I can believe my wife. Guards, do your duty.

[*The* SOLDIERS *stab* CRISPUS.

CRISPUS

God forgive you, Father. I am innocent. (*He dies.*)

CONSTANTINE

Leave me.

[SOLDIERS *and* BASSIANA MARCIA *go out.*

So let the unrighteous perish. . . . Poor Fausta! If you had told me why you hated him I would have acted earlier, and prevented—— And so, perhaps the horror would have survived, to crawl into the throne. Better as it is. . . . Just God, was this well done? To send this corruption into my very blood?

[*Hoofs approaching.*

Has Thy servant deserved no more than to be made a mock to the whole Empire? . . . And how to tell the Empire? The people loved this carrion. . . . Well, it is done.

[*Hoofs arrive, and stop.*

TOGI (*off*)

Let me pass, you fools! I am the Emperor's secretary. . . . Augustus! Augustus! (*He rushes in, and sees the body of* CRISPUS.) Constantine, what have you done?

CONSTANTINE

Justice.

TOGI

Murder.

CONSTANTINE

You have come too late, Togi, to applaud me in the character of Roman Father, avenging the purity of his hearth and home. Or perhaps only in the burlesque role of the elderly dotard cuckolded by his own son.

TOGI

Neither. You were cast for the part of Theseus.

CONSTANTINE

Theseus?

TOGI

Or the husband of Potiphar's wife. Your wife and her tools have tricked you nicely, Constantine. Read that. (*Giving letter.*)

CONSTANTINE

What do you know of it? Were you his pander? . . . Villain and traitor! (*He seizes* TOGI *by the throat.*)

TOGI (*throwing him off*)

Read that, I say, and kill me afterwards. . . . I have ridden with it from Rome—not fast enough, dear God, not fast enough.

CONSTANTINE

"Fausta to Licinius"—what's this? Where did it come from?

TOGI

Your mother's servant stole it from your wife's slave.

CONSTANTINE

O God! (*He staggers to a chair and sits staring at the letter in a kind
of bewilderment.*)

TOGI

I killed two horses under me, and still I came too late. (*He kneels
and closes the eyes of* CRISPUS.) Forgive me, dear Lord Crispus. May
Christ receive your innocent soul.

CONSTANTINE

Innocent.

TOGI

"The souls of the righteous are in the hand of God, and there shall
no torment touch them." Go in peace. (*He folds* CRISPUS' *hands
and arranges the body.*)

CONSTANTINE

"*Ut puto, deus fio*". So said the dying Nero—do you hear that, Togi?
—"I believe I am becoming a god". Well, so I am. I have been
God's vice-gerent so long that now He's promoting me. I am lord
of the world, like God. I had a son, like God, and like God's Son
he was innocent, and I killed him—just like God. I delivered him
up to the soldiers, and they smote him through the side. "And
over his head this accusation written." . . . No, but it's funny,
Togi—can't you see it's funny? . . . All those solemn old grey-
beards in Nicaea, wrangling about God's Son, with me sitting
there on my golden throne—and none of them knew, none of
them knew (*laughing hysterically*) that I was going to sacrifice my
beloved son and be turned into very God!

TOGI (*shaking him roughly*)

Stop that! stop it, I tell you. . . . God indeed! God's vice-gerent!
Nonsense! . . . You're a common sinner like the rest of us, d'you
hear?—an ordinary, stupid headstrong man with a violent
temper, who has committed a common murder. . . . And you
didn't even mean to do it, God help you. . . . Your fault was haste
and folly—that's human enough, Heaven knows.

177

CONSTANTINE

Let go! I am a parricide and my touch is pollution. . . . The
Furies smell the blood upon my hands—what's that, crawling
there on the threshold?

TOGI

Only my cloak. . . . Dear Master, this is no talk for a Christian.
There are no Furies, and how can one fellow-sinner pollute
another? We are all guilty of Christ's death, and all redeemed by
His blood.

CONSTANTINE

Crispus is dead. . . . I loved him.

TOGI

I know you did.

CONSTANTINE

I still can't understand. Who made this plot? Not my wife—say
it was not my wife.

TOGI

They were all in it together. Licinius was the heart, Bassiana
Marcia was the head, I think—but the hand was Fausta's.

CONSTANTINE

What made her do it?

TOGI

As a wife, she was jealous of your work; as a mother she was
jealous for her sons.

CONSTANTINE

You knew—and no one warned me? . . . Don't answer. . . . Livia
warned me. "Traitor's blood", she said. My mother tried to
warn me; she said: "Take care, she is in love with you."

TOGI

It was a kind of love.

CONSTANTINE

And a kind of hatred too. . . . I was stupid. I didn't see, but it's all
clear now. Almost ridiculously clear. (*He is speaking now with a kind
of feverish lucidity.*) Her father killed, her brother killed, her gods
defeated, her husband absorbed in an empire which her sons

might not inherit. And that woman always by her to rub salt into
her wounds.

Togi

That's how it was, God forgive her.

Constantine

"Forgive"—you all say that. *He* said it as he died. But princes
dare not forgive. . . . We are wasting time; we have to consider the
Empire. . . . Let me see. The plot was that I should be tricked into
killing Crispus; that part of it, you see, has succeeded. What next?
Fausta and Bassiana Marcia would swear that my son was innocent. Crassus would raise up Rome in rebellion against the
parricide, while Licinius and Martinianus would march against
Nicomedia from the East. Very pretty. . . . Get ink and paper.
Write.

Togi

Write what, Augustus?

Constantine

The death-warrants. . . . How fortunate that I was never baptised!
I can damn myself with a clear conscience. . . . Take down the
names. Crassus, with his chief confederates—you will find out
who they are. . . . Bassiana Marcia—she is here, under my hand,
most conveniently. The Empress Fausta—she ought to head the
list. Wait! I had forgotten the Vicennalia. "Not on the feast-day,
lest there be an uproar among the people"—I seem to know that
phrase. Write her down, but with stay of execution until after
the Festival. . . . Are my sons implicated?

Togi

God forbid! the eldest is not twelve years old.

Constantine

I must not be a spendthrift of my children. I will consult my
mother. Go on. Martinianus. Licinius. Need I execute my sister
Constantia?

Togi

I think, sir, she had a mind to warn you, but dared not speak
plainly for her husband's sake.

179

CONSTANTINE

Well, let her live. . . . What else?

TOGI

Sir, what announcement is to be made concerning the Lord Crispus?

CONSTANTINE

Anything—except the truth. Say he is dead, but give no reasons. Let people believe what they will—that Fausta's story was true, or that he was involved with Licinius. . . . Don't you see, man, don't you see, that if these plotters can prove their case they may still pull off their rebellion? I have taken my son's life and now I have no choice but to take away his good name. . . . Don't look at me like that—d'you think I like it? If God does not like it, tell Him He should have given you better horses.

TOGI

Constantine, what can I say?

CONSTANTINE

There is nothing to be said and a great deal to be done. Make haste to Rome—tell them that the Emperor is coming. First the solemn thanksgiving, then the bloodshed. We do not call it that— we call it justice. But I think there is no justice, either in earth or Heaven.

[TOGI *goes out, in pitying silence.* CONSTANTINE *remains staring at the dead* CRISPUS *while the shadows fall.*

SCENE 11

A.D. 326—*Rome: a small chapel in the palace, with an altar, and* HELENA, *veiled in black, praying before it. Night.* ($\frac{1}{2}$ *set B.*)

[*Enter* CONSTANTINE, *as from a journey.*

CONSTANTINE

Mother!

HELENA (*rising and going to him*)

My poor child!

CONSTANTINE

Don't pity me; I can't stand that. I am here in Rome, and my business is to rejoice. . . . What were you praying for?

HELENA

For mercy upon all sinners.

CONSTANTINE

You told me once that until I understood sin I should never understand God. Now I know sin—I *am* sin; and understand nothing at all.

HELENA

The sin was not all yours. You were cruelly deceived.

CONSTANTINE

That's not what I mean. Sin is more terrible than you think. It is not lying and cruelty and murder—it is a corruption of life at the source. I and mine are so knit together in evil that no one can tell where the guilt begins or ends. And I who called myself God's emperor—I find now that all my justice is sin and all my mercy bloodshed.

HELENA

You have discovered that? (*She sits down.*)

CONSTANTINE

I murdered Crispus on the day that I spared Licinius. I corrupted Fausta when first I gave shelter to her father, and the hands that clasped her in the bride-bed were set about her throat. I have founded Christ's empire in the grave, and purchased the blood of the martyrs with the slaughter of armies. The clemency of Constantine is more deadly than his vengeance; and if I were to pardon now, more and more deaths would follow. Yet how shall I sit in judgment who am a partner in the crime?

HELENA

You must, my child; that is the bitter portion of princes. It is sin to judge and sin to refrain from judgment, because evil can never be undone, but only purged and redeemed.

CONSTANTINE

Crispus . . . when I saw him lie there dead, I understood how she came to do it. I believe that was the first time I had ever really thought about her. I could almost have forgiven her—but the Empire must not forgive.

HELENA

To forgive and to spare are not always the same. You spared Maximian and Licinius once—did you forgive them?

CONSTANTINE (*surprised by a new idea*)

Why, no—I suppose not. I didn't care for them enough. I wanted to be magnanimous. . . . I see. One can spare and not forgive—and one can also forgive, and not spare. . . . God forgives us—but does he spare us?

HELENA (*sighing*)

Not. very often. He did not spare Himself. The price is always paid, but not always by the guilty.

CONSTANTINE

By whom, then?

HELENA

By the blood of the innocent.

CONSTANTINE

Oh no!

HELENA

By nothing else, my child. Every man's innocence belongs to Christ, and Christ's to him. And innocence alone can pardon without injustice, because it has paid the price.

CONSTANTINE

That is intolerable.

HELENA

It is the hardest thing in the world—to receive salvation at the hand of those we have injured. But if they do not plead for us there is nobody else who can. That is why there is no redemption except in the cross of Christ. For He alone is true God and true Man, wholly innocent and wholly wronged, and we shed His blood every day.

CONSTANTINE

True God out of true God. . . . Athanasius flung the words in Arius' face, and all those old men applauded. (*He falls on his knees before* HELENA.) Mother, tell me, whose blood is on my hands? The blood of Maximian, the blood of Maxentius, of Crassus, Licinius, Marcia, Bassianus, Fausta—the blood of Crispus?

HELENA

The blood of God

[CONSTANTINE *buries his face in her lap.*

which makes intercession for us. . . . Last night in a dream I saw the Cross itself—the very wood which bore the burden of our redemption. I saw how it lay in Jerusalem deep hidden beneath the earth, till the world should be ready to receive it. And a voice said "Seek and find, and the leaves of the tree shall be for the healing of the nations". So then I woke, and remembered my father's words—do *you* remember?

CONSTANTINE

"Air and fire in Gaul, under the earth at Jerusalem"—I had forgotten them till this moment. Yet I saw the sign in Gaul, and believed, or thought I believed.

HELENA

Give me a ship, Constantine; give me a ship and men, so that I may go to Jerusalem and find the Tree of Glory. For the time is come, and the Church is set free, and the world is ready to creep to the foot of the Cross and be healed of its pain.

CONSTANTINE

Take all the ships you want, Mother, and all the men, too. But I am bound and not free, and the iron of the nails is in my very flesh. Pray for me.

HELENA

O holy God, Holy and strong, Holy and Immortal, have mercy upon us. By the wood and the iron, by the wormwood and the gall, by the water and the blood, have mercy upon us.

Innocent Blood of Jesus, plead for us,
Innocent blood of Abel, plead for us,
Innocent blood of Crispus, plead for us,
Blood of the Holy Innocents, plead for us,
All innocent victims, pray for us.

[*The curtain of the chapel is drawn, and the stage remains dark for a moment. Then the new day comes in, gradually flooding every corner of the Palace. The voices of the* CROWD *are heard, off, shouting for the Emperor and Empress.*

Enter, from the opposite side of the stage, FAUSTA *in full Imperial dress, attended.*

FAUSTA

Fulvia.

FULVIA

Madam.

FAUSTA

Go and inform Augustus that I have been ready this half hour. If he did not condescend to visit me on his arrival, that is no reason why he should keep me waiting now. You will find him, no doubt, with the Lady Helena—he has always time for her.

[*Exit* FULVIA.

Where is Bassiana Marcia? Did she not return last night with Augustus?

LADY

I think not, madam.

FAUSTA

Why not? She was commanded to do so. (*A momentary uneasiness passes over her face.*) No matter.

[*Enter* TOGI.

TOGI

Madam, may I beg a word with you in private?

FAUSTA (*signing to her* LADIES *to step back out of earshot*)
Well?

TOGI

Augustus sends this message: Your conspiracy is discovered, your confederates are dead. Yourself are reprieved until after the conclusion of the ceremonies, which, in the public interest, Augustus desires you to carry through in accordance with the programme as arranged.

184

FAUSTA (*reeling a little under the blow, but recovering herself, and disdainfully putting aside his tentative gesture of support— in a half-whisper*)

My children?

TOGI

Their safety, madam, is assured, in dependence upon your good behaviour. Augustus bids me add that, as concerns the wrongs between you and him, he begs that you will forgive him as he forgives you; but that as to the public wrong there can be no remission of the penalty.

FAUSTA

I have no use for forgiveness. As for the rest, I submit to Augustus.

[TOGI *bows and goes. The* LADIES *gather about* FAUSTA. *The young* CAESAR CONSTANTINE *enters with* LACTANTIUS *and comes up to her.*

CONSTANTINE CAESAR

Are we all ready, Mother? When do we start? Where's Father?

FAUSTA

He is coming.

[*She mechanically straightens his laurel chaplet, and stands with her hand on his shoulder.*

Trumpets. From the upper part of the stage, enter CONSTANTINE, *wearing the tunica palmata and toga picta, with diadem and sceptre, and attended by* HELENA, TOGI, *the* OFFICERS *of the* HOUSEHOLD *and by* GENERALS, SOLDIERS, *etc. with the Labarum. As he advances,* FAUSTA *takes her place beside him, and like a pair of magnificent automata the Imperial Pair pass out with their train to be greeted by the jubilant shouts of the City.*

THE EPILOGUE

[*A* PRIEST *enters:* TOGI *comes out to him through the door.*

TOGI

You are from Athanasius?

PRIEST

From Athanasius, exiled in Gaul. He has sent me with a message to the Emperor.

TOGI

The Emperor is dying.

PRIEST

I feared as much, from what I heard in the town. Athanasius will be grieved, for in spite of all that has happened, he loves Augustus. . . . Are you not the Secretary Togius? . . . I saw you at Nicaea, twelve years ago, when I came to the Great Council with Bishop Alexander, on whom be peace.

TOGI

Amen. Those twelve years have seen many changes.

PRIEST

Yes, indeed. Alexander dead, Hosius dead, the good Lady Helena, too, gone to her blessed rest. Arius dead by the judgment of God, Eustathius of Antioch condemned for heresy, Athanasius banished for his resolute defence of the Faith.

TOGI

Do not blame Augustus too much for that, He supported him against many attacks. But these prolonged quarrels in the Church disappointed him, till in the end he lost heart and temper.

PRIEST

Some say that he was never the same man after that matter of the Lord Crispus.

TOGI

Maybe. God have mercy upon all sinners.

PRIEST

Amen. . . . And now he is dying. Is he dying in the Faith?

TOGI

Yes. The Bishop is with him now to baptise him and to receive him into the fold of Christ's Church. . . . Will you come in? You may stand with the Household in the ante-chamber.

PRIEST

Most willingly. . . . Tomorrow is Whitsun Day—a blessed Pentecost for Constantine, and for all of us.

[*They pass in. The curtain is drawn aside to show a room or chapel with* CONSTANTINE *lying sick upon his bed, and* EUSEBIUS *with other* BISHOPS *and* PRIESTS *preparing to baptise him from a font of water. They have just removed his Imperial robes, that they may clothe him in the white chrisom of the neophyte.*

CONSTANTINE

Put away the purple—I shall never wear it again. Christ's robe alone, white and unspotted. . . . Togi!

TOGI

Here, my dear lord.

CONSTANTINE

Give us room.

[*Priests move back.*

. . . They are all gone but you; nobody else living knows the truth about——

TOGI

About that night at Pola.

CONSTANTINE

I have confessed my part in it, and the Church will be silent. When I am gone, do you keep the secrets of the dead.

TOGI

I will.

187

CONSTANTINE

If men think me still more guilty than I am, I am content. It is my only share in the innocent blood, and little enough, God knows. . . . Where is Athanasius?

TOGI

In Treves, my lord.

CONSTANTINE

Ask him to forgive me. I came to dread the sight of him. He reminded me too much that the blood I had shed was God's blood. But I now accept that most terrible truth as the sole hope of salvation. Tell him so.

TOGI

I will tell him.

CONSTANTINE

Let us now put off all dissimulation, stripped naked to the cleansing waters. . . . Eusebius!

[EUSEBIUS, *with the* PRIESTS, *returns to the bed.*

Are you there? I can't see very well. Everything is getting confused.

TOGI (*in a low tone*)

Make haste, my Father; the fever is returning upon him.

EUSEBIUS (*reading the baptismal service*)

"Blessed is the Kingdom of the Father, of the Son, and of the Holy Ghost always, now and ever, and unto ages of ages. . . ."

[*As the service proceeds, the* VOICE OF COEL *mingles with and overtops that of* EUSEBIUS, *and on the darkened stage the Vision of the Past appears, beginning with the form of* COEL *himself.*

COEL

Coel the son of Coel the son of Coel the heaven-born;
I have harped in the Twelve Houses, I have prophesied among the
                                                    Dancers,
Coel, father of the Light who bears the Sun in her bosom.

Three times have I seen the Cross:
Air and fire in Gaul;

> [*The sign of the Chi-Ro appears.*

                              under the earth in Jerusalem

> [HELENA *appears, carrying the Cross.*

Written upon water in the place of the victories.

EUSEBIUS

"Wherefore, O merciful King, be present with us now by the indwelling of Thy Holy Spirit. (*He breathes upon the water.*) Sanctify this water and give to it the grace of redemption, the blessing of Jordan. (*He signs the water three times with the cross.*) By the sign of the precious cross let all adverse powers be shattered. . . ."

COEL

Three times have I heard the Word:
The Word in a dream,

> [*The words "Hoc signo victor eris" appear about the Chi-Ro.*

                              the word in council,

> [*The* BISHOPS *of Nicaea appear.*

The word of the Word amid the courts of the Trinity.

> [ATHANASIUS *appears with the Book of the Gospels.*

Three crowns: laurel among the trumpets,

> [*The* ARMIES *appear.*

A diadem of stars with fillets of purple,

> [*The head of* MAXENTIUS *appears, crowned with the diadem.*

Thorns and gold for the Bride of the Trinity.

> [*The* CHURCH *appears beneath the sign of the Chi-Ro.*

I have seen Constantine in the air as a flying eagle,

> [*The Roman eagles and the Labarum appear, with their standard-bearer.*

I have seen Constantine in the earth as a raging lion,

> [CRISPUS *and* FAUSTA *appear, with other persons slain by* CONSTANTINE.

Dost thou believe on Christ?

CONSTANTINE

I believe on Him as King and God, and worship Father, Son, and Holy Ghost, consubstantial and undivided Trinity.

COEL

I have seen Constantine in the water as a swimming fish.

EUSEBIUS (*pouring the water three times upon* CONSTANTINE)

"The servant of God, Constantine, is baptised in the name of the Father, Amen, and of the Son, Amen, and of the Holy Ghost, Amen."

COEL

Earth and water and air—but the beginning and the ending is fire;
Light in the first day, fire in the last day, at the coming of the
Word;
And Our Lord the Spirit descending in light and in fire.

[*As he speaks, the Vision fades, the Chi-Ro and the* CHURCH *remaining to the last. When these too have faded, the stage remains dark for a few moments. Then four tall candles are seen to be carried in and set at the head and foot of the bed. As the light returns, we see* CONSTANTINE *lying dead, with the candles about him, the* CHURCH *standing at his head.*

THE CHURCH

I believe in One God;

VOICES (*in the darkness, gradually gathering in number and strength*)

The Father almighty, Maker of Heaven and earth, and of all things visible and invisible. And in one Lord Jesus Christ, the only-begotten Son of God, begotten of His Father before all worlds. God of God; Light of Light; Very God of Very God; begotten, not made; being of one substance with the Father; by whom all things were made. Who for us men and for our salvation came down from Heaven. . . .

CURTAIN

A BRIEF BIBLIOGRAPHY

Eusebius of Caesarea: *Vita Constantini.*

Cambridge Ancient History, Vol. XII.

A. H. M. Jones: *Constantine and the Conversion of Europe.*

A. Alföldi: *The Conversion of Constantine and Pagan Rome.*

J. Palanque, G. Bardy, and P. de Labriolle: *The Church in the Christian Roman Empire.*

A. E. Burn: *The Council of Nicaea.*

F. W. Farrar: *Lives of the Fathers,* Vol. I.

G. L. Prestige: *God in Patristic Thought.*

G. L. Prestige: *Fathers and Heretics.*

C. N. Cochrane: *Christianity and Classical Culture.*